THE
BROKEN HARP

Identity and Language
in Modern Ireland

Tomás Mac Síomóin

Nuascéalta

NOTE

The content of *The Broken Harp* is an extension of material discussed originally in the following publications: *1916: Leath-réabhlóid–Paradacsa Ait na Gaeilge* (2006),*Ó Mhársa go Magla* (2006) and most particularly, in *Nua-Éireannachas–Namhad don Ghaeilge?* and *Féiniúlacht, Cultúr agus Teanga i Ré an Domhandaithe* (2011). These texts by Tomás Mac Síomóin were published by Coiscéim Teoranta.

.

CONTENTS

ACKNOWLEDGMENTS

I am greatly indebted to Jenny Farrell, Renate Mitchell, and Éamon Ó Ciosáin, who read the original manuscript of *The Broken Harp* and whose corrections, contributions and helpful suggestions are integrated into the present text, to Cathal Mac Gabhann for suggesting the work in the first place, to Conchúr Ó Giollagáin for his many useful comments and to Jean Le Dû, from whose comprehensive critique *The Broken Harp* greatly benefited.

I am solely responsible for the opinions and ideas expressed in *The Broken Harp*.

Díbhse uilig, mo mhíle buíochas!

The harp that once through Tara's halls
The soul of music shed,
Now hangs as mute on Tara's walls
As if that soul were fled...

Thomas Moore (1779-1852)

INTRODUCTION

In the Shakespearean play, *Henry V*, probably written about 1599, Captain Macmorris, an Irish officer in an English army invading France, is clearly viewed with suspicion. A Welsh captain refers to Ireland as "your nation" while questioning his leadership abilities. Macmorris' answer indicates his confused national orientation:

"Of my nation! What ish my nation? Ish a villain and a bastard and a knave and a rascal. What ish my nation? Who talks of my nation? I do not know you so good a man as myself. So Chrish save me I will cut off your head."

This only voice of Ireland in Shakespeare, an angry one at that, in an imagined Gaelic Irish accent lampooned by the playwright, gives to understand that Ireland was, through the eyes of the Bard of Stratford Upon Avon, part of the English nation. Macmorris, a truly colonized subject, responds angrily when his pertinence to that nation is questioned and he is made to feel like a rank outsider to it. In his anger he betrays frustration at the English stereotyping of his own people as villains, bastards, knaves and rascals.

Macmorris' reaction reflects an incipient identity crisis that seems to have affected some Gaelic Irish, especially (but not exclusively) those of probable Old

English provenance, like Macmorris himself, even before the 16th Century Tudor reconquest of Ireland was completed and the subsequent precipitous Gaelic decline, had yet to manifest itself.

But what does the plaintive *"What ish my nation?"* mean today? Some would argue that the question has but marginal relevancy at most in a world where traditional national boundaries are increasingly blurred. For, a salient fact of the world we live in is that Anglophone monoculture, accompanying the current galloping internationalization of trade and commerce, erases cultural boundaries wherever it establishes itself. Nowhere is this observation more apposite than in today's Ireland.

Nevertheless, Macmorris's centuries-old question is still asked, both in "Erin's Green Isle" and in "the greater Ireland beyond the seas". Why this recurrent obsession of the Irish with the condition of Irishness, almost 100 years after the 1916 Rising, the foundational act of Irish independence? Especially since most other peoples, secure in their sense of national identity, are untroubled by such questions.

A basic indicator of the Hibernian condition for most to-the-manner-born, is having Irish-accented English. Or, the fact of having been born in Ireland! Or having Irish-born ancestors! Or being a citizen of the Republic of Ireland! Or sharing a specifically Irish set of historical or cultural referents! For some, profession of the Roman Catholic religion is a *sine qua non* of Irishness.

Ancillary, and more ephemeral, signs of Irishness

can be loyalty to the national sporting teams, to the Gaelic Athletic Association, to certain singers and their music, Irish dancing, etc. Some would see that having the "gift of the gab"—the ability to string together a long list of humorous anecdotes, reminiscences and opinions—as an almost uniquely Irish attribute.

For a tiny minority, the ability to speak Irish Gaelic, the first official language of the Republic of Ireland, is at the core of its Irishness. However, the majority of present-day Irish citizens probably feel that the ability to speak Irish, which many may even see, paradoxically, as being foreign, can no longer be a defining national characteristic. Their Irishness is expressed fully and completely through English. Loss of the ancestral tongue is often seen by them, where considered at all (which is seldom), as the inevitable price of societal modernization. Can such attitudes afford us a vital clue as we seek to unravel the complexity of contemporary Irishness?

Outside observers may attribute attitudinal and behavioral idiosyncrasies of the Irish (being the "*men that God made mad*", according to G.K. Chesterton), to our mild soft climate, our romantic anti-materialistic nature, our fiery "Celtic" temperament, our innate tendency to fantasize (oft-proclaimed perennial bedrock of our famous literary culture), our personal warmth ("*the friendliest people on earth*" according to tourist bumph of recent vintage) and, of course, that strong Roman Catholic faith that sustained us through all our people's many and various vicissitudes.

Less endearing Irish characteristics abound: our

"Celtic" melancholy, conformity to externally concocted stereotypes (e.g. the drunken Paddy, etc.), sexual prudery, emotional coldness, violence, alcoholism, our widespread dislike of most non-Anglophone peoples, our shamefaced refusal to renew our own historic cultural identity, our innate social/political conservatism/submissiveness, etc.

All of these traits, and more, can be conveniently trivialized by being attributed to Ireland's glowering grey skies and damp climate, a too free dalliance with the demon drink, our puritanical Roman Catholicism (inherited largely from Victorian England), and, of course, the shrewd peasant pragmatism at the core of Irish leprechaunery.

The seldom considered possibility that these characteristics, and others, can be seen as a more or less inevitable outcome of the particularities of Irish history are at the core of *The Broken Harp*.

The behavioral profile of the present-day Irish population contrasts with the apparent administrative normality of the Republic of Ireland, ostensibly a fully functional modern state and member of both the United Nations and a European Union led by a group of ex-colonial powers. However, considering the relevant data, we will find that said profile conforms more closely to the condition of colonized indigenous peoples around the globe than those of the populations that colonized them, among whom figure many of our new European partners.

Furthermore, research on the offspring of victims of colonial and other brutality indicates, unexpectedly, that the psychological effects of such trauma are genetically transmissible. Thence it is hypothesized in *The Broken Harp* that the Irish historical experience—as is the proven case with other traumatized peoples—is inscribed, at least partially, in the DNA or epigenetic profile, or both, of past and current Irish populations.

Thus, convincing explanations of some attitudes and behavior considered to be "typically Irish" are more likely to derive, at least partly, from genetic/epigenetic and neurobiological studies as from a perspective through which a cultural transgenerational transmission of behavioral traits is the sole mechanism visualized.

This enquiry conducts us into areas not usually traversed by cultural inquirers, whose curiosity is often diverted by romantic nationalism's myths or their antinationalist converse. Skirting such well-trodden byways and the dense polysyllabic thickets of postcolonial theory, we will cover some less familiar terrain to try and resolve credibly the elusive conundrum of contemporary Irishness: why the Irish are the way they are, and why they aren't the way they are not.

This modest journalistic enterprise does not pretend to be exhaustive nor is it the densely referenced bulky tome its subject merits. Not every idea or fact therein is referenced, though most are. Nor are sources always provided for facts that can be confirmed easily through a keyboard search. The enterprise takes the form of a series of interlocking and sometimes overlapping reflections, not always in strict linear sequence.

Appendices to the essay deal with the possibility,

or not, of reviving Irish and the decline of Irish-language literary culture.

Some of the most illuminating clues encountered in this search are of an unavoidably technical nature; we will do our best to present this information in terms Seán and Mary Citizen can understand.

Tomás Mac Síomóin,
Sant Feliu de Guíxols,
09/11/2014.

THE IRISH
AND THEIR ANCESTRAL LANGUAGE

MOTHER TONGUE

Discussion of the current situation of the Irish language is apposite to this enquiry. For, how the Irish value a cultural artifact that is exclusively theirs, their ancestral tongue, can afford us valuable clues both as to how they value their traditional identity and how that valuation mutated in response to historical circumstance. Consideration of such linguistic mutations, how they originated, together with their cultural, social and psychological implications and consequences, form a substantial part of the body of this work.

Analysis of the present situation of the Irish language is a convenient starting point for such a reflection.

To state it simply: the prognosis for Irish is not good. Of the more than 6000 languages spoken around the globe, linguistic experts reckon that, thanks to the domination of a handful of major languages, between 50% and 90% of languages spoken at the beginning of the twenty-first century will have vanished by the year 2100.

If the current pattern of Irish Gaelic usage continues, a comprehensive sociolinguistic study conducted by NUI-Galway researchers, and published in 2007, shows that Irish as a community language, communal Irish, will be extinct within a few short years!

Is this demise really important? The great Kenyan

novelist and cultural activist, Ngũgĩ wa Thiong'o (b. Kamirithu, Kenya, 1938), who switched from writing in English to his native Kikuyu/Gikuyu, affirms language and culture to be "*almost indistinguishable*"; thence, in his view, the death of a language and the culture it bears within it are necessarily coincidental:

"Communication between human beings is the basis and process of evolving culture. Values are the basis of people's identity, their sense of particularity as members of the human race. All this is carried by language. Language as culture is the collective memory bank of a people's experience in history. Culture is almost indistinguishable from the language that makes possible its genesis, growth, banking, articulation and indeed its transmission from one generation to the next."

So, in Thiong'o's lexicon, the loss of the Irish language means the ultimate shedding of what little remains of the historic identity of the Irish people.

If that were, in fact, the case, the results of the 2007 survey[*],that clearly signals the imminent end of Irish as a community language, should have seriously concerned not only Irish-language activists, administrators and academics but all concerned with the cultural course of the Irish nation. Recent publications of Conchúr Ó Giollagáin, director of the 2007 survey, point once again to such a linguicide.

---

[*]*Comprehensive Linguistic Study of the Use of Irish in the Gaeltacht: Principal Findings and Recommendations, 2007.*

Such concern is far from being the case, however. Nor has it been the case for most Irish people, for whom the fortunes of the Irish language are of little interest.

Yet, *Gaeilge* is, according to the Constitution, the first language of the Republic of Ireland. Vox-pop surveys show that a substantial majority of the population of the Republic "cherishes" the language. However this is the same majority that has been exposed to Irish lessons at school for at least twelve years, without being able—or willing—to acquire, in the overwhelming majority of cases, even the most rudimentary speaking knowledge of that language.

Why this seeming contradiction of a people rejecting a language that is uniquely theirs? And what is the nature of the mental/psychological block that inhibits even the minority that acquires an elementary knowledge of Irish from speaking this language and, thus, improving their ability to do so? And, importantly, whence this obvious aversion?

Thus, the hostility of his late 20th century Dublin neighbors and peers towards the young Irish-speaking Hugo Hamilton and his language, as recounted by him in his autobiographical *The Speckled People* is, far from being an exceptional case. The visceral hatred of Irish by some Galway natives is described graphically by Pádraig Ó'Toole in his autobiography, *Aran to Africa* (Nuascéalta, 2013). Irish-speakers who are brusquely refused their right to service through Irish in Government offices and agencies will have their own stories to tell.

Can this contradiction, the Irish rejecting in practice their "cherished" traditional language, signal the underlying nature of today's Irishness? I believe so. Especially when we consider this anomaly in tandem with the other aspects of the Irish condition we will be discussing in the course of this essay.

THERE'LL ALWAYS BE A *GAELTACHT*?

But first let us get an objective handle on the reality of the Irish language situation in the few remaining areas where it is still spoken!

The comprehensive 2007 socio-linguistic study of the use of Irish in Irish-speaking districts, known collectively as the *Gaeltacht*, concludes that the language will cease to be used there, both domestically and publicly, within 15-20 years, even in those districts where the language is strongest. So the time frame indicated by the study has now shrunk to 8–13 years.

This unnoticed and unlamented death of the dominant community language in Ireland for over 2000 years, underlines the total failure of all efforts heretofore to restore Irish as the common language of Irish citizens. This has been both the basic aim of the Language Revival Movement for over a century and was a stated aim of Irish State policy for more than a generation after the country achieved partial independence in 1922.

However, given the increasing integration of Ireland, both culturally and socially, into the neo-liberal global economy via membership of the EU—and its current enthusiastic espousal of Anglophone media—the present likelihood of a serious re-commitment to such a linguistic aim is miniscule, to be as optimistic as is humanly possible under such prevailing circumstances.

But---and all objective evidence to the contrary— there will always be a *Gaeltacht* to salve the national conscience, even when it has become abstract and insipidly aspirational, morphing into a quasi-living folk museum. Did transfer of the administration of the latter entity to the Department of Arts, Heritage and the *Gaeltacht* from a specific Department of the *Gaeltacht* amount to a not so subliminal recognition of that reality?

SEE NO EVIL, HEAR NO EVIL!

A very common reaction of ordinary Irish speakers to the evidence presented in the aforementioned study of Irish usage in the *Gaeltacht* is to ignore its findings or to obstinately refuse to believe that the future of communal Irish could ever be endangered. They often opine that, in any case, the work of *Gaelscoileanna* (Irish-medium schools) guarantees the survival of the Irish language well into the 21st century. See no evil, *a chara*, hear no evil…

Accordingly, the little that there is of conscience regarding this matter having been so easily assuaged, very little impetus comes from within "Gaeldom" (the little that remains, within the *Gaeltacht* and without, of the Irish-speaking "world") to define, and work towards, whatever transformation of the social and cultural status quo that might be deemed necessary to prevent the extinction of communal Irish.

So, what is it in the *Gaeilgeoir* (Irish speaker) psyche that enables it to live comfortably and unconcernedly in the egregious contradiction that exists between the reality of the present endangered situation of the Irish language and his frequently casually optimistic perception of that reality?

Can we gain further insight into the relation the Irish have with their language and identity by considering the linguistic praxis of young native Irish speakers themselves with regard to their own language?

GÉARLA TRUMPS *GAEILGE*

One outstanding contradiction leaps out of that *Gaeltacht* survey to which we have referred. Namely, while 53% of school pupils are being reared through Irish in one of the strongest *Gaeltacht* districts, only 24% of them converse with their peers through the medium of that language.

The reason for this somewhat startling anomaly would seem to be that *Gaeltacht* youth can better communicate their concerns through English rather than Irish, which they sense to lack the registers needed to adequately express the contemporary concerns of their age-group. Some sociolinguists who study *Gaeltacht* language usage tell me that all *Gaeltacht* residents under the age of 40 speak better English than Irish.

Some *Gaeltacht* residents may contest this claim,

but it is clear that the language of the vast majority of young native speakers has evolved, "stagnated" is perhaps the more appropriate word, into what they describe as a *teanga easnamhach* (an incomplete language). The latter is a syntactical, lexicographical and phonetic mixture of Irish and English that would be well-nigh incomprehensible to monoglot native Irish speakers of only 40 years ago...

Examples of *Géarla*, (i.e. *Gaeilge+Béarla*), the term used in this essay to identify this syncretic hybrid speech, abound in *An Chonair Chaoch* (ACC), an illuminating series of papers in which current *Gaeltacht* school-goer speech is recorded and analyzed.

The extent to which *Géarla* violates the syntax, vocabulary and even the phonetic norms of the *teanga iomlán* (complete language), reflects the overwhelming cultural and linguistic presence of English in districts where Irish was unchallenged only a generation ago.

Géarla is seen as a linguistic half-way house by sociolinguists. It is abundantly clear from the speech samples presented in ACC that many of its informants think in English while they struggle to express their thoughts in Irish. Such confusion and its results are not unique to Irish.

Dying languages everywhere have their *Géarlas*. For example, Nancy Dorian, an American linguist who studied the decline of Scottish Gaelic in East Sutherland, where the language is, in 2014, down to 3 remaining native speakers (there were 200 in 1963), recorded many such "linguistic half-way houses" there, whose presence was a clear indication that the old language was dying while giving way to the new.

As previously mentioned, zealous language enthusiasts often claim that *Gaeltacht* language loss is now compensated for by the increasing number of *Gaelscoileanna* (Irish-medium schools) graduates. However, in spite of the dedicated work of many teachers, such learned Irish turns out to be—with rare exceptions—another *teanga easnamhach*, sometimes on a par with that of many of today's young *Gaeltacht* Irish speakers.

Géarla is inadequate to accessing most discourses in Irish, even those of less than moderate sophistication. Access to literature in complete Irish, the language of their grandparents (in the case of *Gaeltacht* youth), by such students is impossible without the continuing aid of a dictionary, a recourse seldom availed of.[*]

The weakness of modern Irish literary culture, along with its implications, is discussed in Appendix II (p.214), is due, in large measure to this inability to read Irish with facility. This in turn also affects the

---

[*]Criticism in this section of the results of *Gaelscoil* tuition does not imply that the *Gaelscoileanna* movement should be abandoned. The "half-way house" of *Gaelscoil Géarla* may serve in some cases as a stepping stone to possession of the complete language and its culture, or as near thereto as is possible under present conditions. But the efficiency of this process could be facilitated, probably, by a smaller number of *Gaelscoileanna* and a more rigorous discrimination on linguistic grounds regarding student admission and staff employment. For this to happen, the *Gaelscoileanna* would require an opt-out from the current Department of Education student admission protocol which is based on the applicant's living in the *Gaelscoil*'s catchment area rather than on his/hers previous knowledge of Irish, e.g., or the parent's genuine interest in their offspring's acquisition of the language.

spoken language. For, a literary culture serves not only to reflect a spoken language but also, in some significant measure to enrich, and both amplify and configure the boundaries of demotic speech.

Semiliterate *Géarla* speakers/readers are thus trapped in a double bind. Their inability/unwillingness to access "complete Irish" texts perpetuates this very inability, thus blocking the possibility of their own transition from *Géarla* to *Gaeilge*.

Then again, many *Géarla* speakers perceive Irish-language literature to be innately "out of synch" with modern Irishness and the present vogue for escapist literature, hence hardly worthy of serious attention. (This somewhat anomalous perception is of a piece with self-castigating attitudes developed by the Irish people during its history, which will be related later in this essay to its lengthy historical experience as an English colonial fiefdom.)

This unwillingness to access Irish language literature may be accentuated, in some cases, by the fact that some *Géarla* speakers are less than enthusiastic learners of Irish, being the end result of parental pressure to have them enrolled in a Gaelscoil. The latter have become to a certain extent victims of their own academic successes; ambitious parents, often with no interest whatsoever in Irish, seeking—understandably—the best possible general education for their children, often try to get them accepted by *Gaelscoileanna*.

Meanwhile, the overwhelmingly Anglophone ambience of modern Ireland continuously augments the English-language component of *Géarla*. It is a matter of common observation that such an unsatisfactory communicative medium is abandoned eventually, by a majority of *Géarla* speakers. Most non-native speaking Gaelscoil alumni quickly abandon *Géarla* for the comfort and flexibility of their mother-tongue, English. Similar patterns of language loss occur in the *Gaeltacht*.

Teenagers who speak English with fellow native speakers will be most unlikely under current and likely future conditions to speak Irish with their fellows when they become adults.

Unspoken languages quickly cease to be known, a fact to which the level of knowledge of Irish in areas that have ceased to become *Gaeltachtaí* within living memory can readily attest.

THE MYSTERIOUS SENSE OF "IN FAVOR"

Yet, most surprisingly, in spite of their verified disinclination to speak Irish with their peers, 94% of *Gaeltacht* youth were "strongly or moderately in favor of the Irish language". What sense are we to make of such a contradiction?

Does this "94% in favor of Irish" offer a ray of hope for the survival of the language beyond a time horizon that looms ever closer? Will the wish, if not just an empty emotional-nostalgic desideratum, be mother to a redemptive linguistic deed? Or, could it be that the ambivalence towards the language that the said 94% demonstrates is joined at the hip to the many vox-pop surveys that indicate that a clear majority of the State's citizens is "in favor of Irish", whatever occult meaning is packaged by that patriotic nostrum?

Yet, although this latter mantra is often repeated by "official" language revivalists, neither god nor devil seems able to impel the same "favorably-disposed towards Irish" masses to speak the very language they claim to favor. One would need to be remarkably non-perceptive in Ireland not to realize that only a tiny percentage of citizens ever learn how to effectively communicate through Irish. Reliable anecdotal evidence points even to the reluctance of the vast majority of the parents of Gaelscoil students to attend special Irish classes offered to them that would enable them to involve themselves meaningfully in their children's homework.

So, whence this strange contradictory attitude towards Irish, evidenced by both Irish and English speakers? And, then again, why do most children of non-nationals not have that block against learning Irish that so afflicts their Irish classmates? (Again, this observation, based on conversations with primary teachers, is anecdotal, but it surely merits further study).

What can this "love" for a language, the speaking of which is rejected in practice, tell us about its non-speaker "devotees"? And, if the language is not really cherished, why pretend that it is so? What does it tell us about contemporary Irishness that the beloved and "cherished" ancestral tongue is kept locked away, almost out of sight and sound, in some isolated "Peig's Corner" from which no escape to a wider social milieu seems possible? Like some doddering deranged elderly aunt of embarrassingly anti-social habits who is kept well out of harm's way as the family forgathers to celebrate its anniversaries or mourn its demises.

What is the meaning of this contradiction, shared by "patriot" and "shoneen" (i.e. an Irish imitator of English ways, from the Irish *seóinín*, little John) alike, that definitively blocks any seriously significant re-emergence of Irish, be it *Gaeilge* or *Géarla*, in Ireland's cultural/linguistic landscape.

In short, how has this shamefaced rejection of the ancestral tongue come to be an almost always unacknowledged but yet, inevitably, an integral part of the essence of contemporary Irishness?

Yet, the fact that the "language question", which splutters into heated expression every so often in the correspondence columns of Ireland's daily newspapers, presses obviously on the raw nerve of a significant number of Irish people must have some psychological significance. If so, what could that significance possibly be?

Let us see if some credible answers to these questions may be found by interrogating some seldom visited corners of Irish history, *"the nightmare from which I am trying to escape"*, in the words of James Joyce's Stephen Dedalus ?

THE ROOT OF IRISHNESS?

To appreciate why the revival of the Irish language is now considered to be a no-go area for most of today's Irish people, we need to consider the roots of contemporary Post-Gaelic Irishness, what will be called here "Super-Colonized Irishness" (SCI), a provisional acronym, selected for reasons that will become obvious later in this essay.

The term "Anglo-Irish" has been pre-empted long ago by a minority stratum of the current Irish population: the descendants of the original colonial settler class, their descendants and, occasionally, their successful native imitators.

What SCI refers to is that cultural/behavioral complex (SCIS, SCI Syndrome) that evolved from Daedalus' "nightmare", from crushing military defeats, genocide, starvation, emigration, cultural and religious persecution, along with language loss, that accompanied the forcible imposition of centuries of English colonial rule on the Irish people. This complex, of which the linguistic ambivalence we have just been discussing is an integral part, still continues to bind us together as a more or less distinctive ethnic entity (though, perhaps, rather "less" than "more" with the passage of time).

The nature and evolution of SCIS can only be profitably understood by considering the historical matrix from which it sprang. However, comparison with other indigenous societies, where similar conditions of brutal colonization prevailed in their recent historic pasts, can help us to amplify this understanding.

But how could such poking into the entrails of our collective past yield results of any practical contemporary relevance?

Wouldn't it just reopen old wounds, generate rancor and nationalistic negativity, just at a time when the Republic of Ireland is embarking on a "new relationship" (or a refurbishing of the old colonial nexus?) with the United Kingdom?

And how can such a raking over of almost dead coals, such as the exercise of dredging up of old unsettled national scores from history's best-forgotten depths, have any place in our electronically integrated global societies, in which the very concepts of nationality and national sovereignty founded on once-shared historical referents itself are losing their traditional relevance?

The old Delphic maxim, *Gnothi Seauton* ("Know Yourself"), oft-quoted by Plato's Socrates, intimates that such self-knowledge as may emerge from the latter examination, having its intrinsic value, is its own justification. But could it have any pragmatic value?

Only from a point of view that sees cultural heterogeneity as a desideratum in itself and, thus being its own justification!

Many cultural observers see global monoculture as the harbinger of an unprecedented cultural impoverishment on a global scale. From that point of view, the battle to maintain and develop the input of humanity's rich tapestry of national languages and cultures, including Irish, must be joined if mankind is to conserve this array of unique founts of cultural and intellectual creativity. And not surrender to the glittering monotony of that global *monothink* and *monofeel*, which is hurrying mankind's older traditions and lesser-used languages to the rubbish heap of history.

From this perspective, if the basis of the present public rejection of Irish is not comprehensively understood, it is most improbable that viable strategies to save this language and its unique cultural potential from certain extinction can even be conceived. From the narrowly pragmatic "economistic" perspective, of course, the amount of energy and expense involved in undoing the linguistic fruits of what is seen as an irreversible historical process has no reasonable justification.

Another caveat invoked by naysayers (to language revival) is that a successful strategy to assure the future of any endangered language in as terminal a situation as Irish has never yet been formulated anywhere, still less carried through successfully. In that context, the very possibility of such a strategy is still very much a moot point. Thence, the enormous effort involved in such a dubious enterprise is hardly justifiable. We will consider this question in some detail in Appendix I (p. 173).

FEAMAINN IS NOT SEAWEED

The primacy of a recognizably Hibernian-accented form of the English language, with its characteristic idiomatic idiosyncrasies, constitutes the essential linguistic dimension of Post-Gaelic Irishness.

"And so what?" asks Paddy the Irishman, "I haven't a word of Irish and I'm just as Irish as you are..." Let us "unpack" this statement, which expresses a common sentiment of most inhabitants of Anglophone Ireland!

Subtending indifference to the linguistic dimension of nationhood is the underlying notion that different languages consist, basically, of readily interchangeable exchangeable systems of cyphers. Thus, from this perspective, one can be as fully Irish, culturally speaking, as a notional monoglot Irish speaker while knowing only English. "Sure what else am I speaking to you but Irish," as a Dublin taxi driver said to me once, "only with English words?"

Few linguists today—and, still less, translators—would agree with this stance. "Seaweed", for example, is not the exact equivalent of *"feamainn"*, which comes with its own unique set of social and literary allusions. This observation can be extended to cover a significant part of the vocabulary of any language, the unique world view, encapsulated by that language, being the end result of the history, social, political etc., of the group that speaks it. This conception found expression in the Sapir-Whorf Hypothesis, well-known to linguists.

Scholars who have considered the linguistic dimension of the colonizing process in detail clearly identify adoption by the colonized subject of the colonizer's language as the defining colonizing moment: that moment when the colonizer's world view superimposes itself on that of the colonized subject.

It may be instructive here to briefly hear how some kindred voices from other parts of the globe express themselves on the cultural significance of this language shift.

The critical role of language in colonization (and decolonization) has also been studied minutely by Filipino scholars. After the violent suppression of the Filipinos by the U.S. in the Filipino-American War of 1898 – 1902, U.S. colonialism, as described by the noted E. San Juan, Jr., harnessed the educational system of the Philippines to the "benevolent" assimilation, i.e. Americanization, of that archipelago.

(This strategy resonates with 19th century educational developments in Ireland, where the British colonial authorities established a national school system in 1831 and used it to linguistically anglicize the Irish population. This system completed work already initiated by clandestine folk "hedge schools", organized by the Irish people themselves to circumvent a Penal Law that denied their right to a Catholic education.)

"The idiom of American English displaced both Spanish and the vernaculars as the primary symbolic system through which Filipinos represented themselves, that is, constituted themselves as colonial subjects with specific positions or functions (rights, duties) in the given social order. It was through this hegemonic language that the colonized subjects, especially the organic intellectuals of the emerging middle strata (merchants, professionals and rich peasants) represented their subordination and validated their serviceability to the norms and projects of the U.S. imperial dispensation.

The Filipino historian, Renato Constantino emphasizes this use of the ruler's language as the root-cause of the Filipino's inveterate self-alienation: 'The first and perhaps the master stroke in the plan to use education as an instrument of colonial policy was the decision to use English as the medium of instruction. English became the wedge that separated the Filipinos from their past and later was to separate educated Filipinos from the masses of their countrymen.' In short, the implantation of U.S. imperial ideology in the Filipino psyche and the routine of everyday life cannot be dissociated from the use of English in business, government, education, and media; this instrumentality of language acted as the synthesizing force that unified a repertoire of social practices through which the public and private identity of the Filipino as 'bearer' of a commodity (labor power) was constituted and subsequently valorized. (i.e. as a subjugated colonized subject who free to dispose of his labor power in the market place)."

Viewed from this perspective, the question of language—of replacing English with a "national" language—appears today as the most crucial site of cultural-political struggle in the Philippines.

In their *Neo-Colonial Politics and Language Struggle in the Philippines* (1984), Virgilio G. Enriquez and Elizabeth Protacio-Marcelino advance the view that possession of a national language is an essential precondition for autonomy. They assert that the continued use of English in a U.S.-oriented educational system (textbooks, curriculum, methodology, etc.):

"...undermines Filipino values and orientation and perpetuates the captivity in the minds of the Filipino people to the colonial outlook. For them, the English language symbolizes the belief in the superiority of U.S. culture, values, society; thus it can only serve the exploitative profit-seeking ends of U.S. power."

This stance with respect to language led to the following policy shift:

"The Constitutional Convention of 1986 agreed to reaffirm 'Filipino' (officially standardized Tagalog)...as the evolving national language of the land...Although English continues to be used predominantly in business and in Government, Filipino-in-the-making as propagated by the mass media—television, films, radio—has practically become the lingua franca throughout the islands. A systematic program of replacing English with Filipino in all universities is now under way so that within the next two or three decades the use of English as the traditionally sanctioned medium of intellectual communication will be gradually phased out."

It should be mentioned here that speakers of other languages native to the Philippine Archipelago other than Tagalog are not at all happy with the elevation of only the latter to the status of "national language".

Ngũgĩ wa Thiong'o has always been a doughty defender of his nation's linguistic rights. His position on the relationship between decolonization and language, as outlined in *The Language of African Literature* from his magisterial *Decolonising the Mind,* is reminiscent of Douglas Hyde's stance regarding Ireland's English-language nationalists, as expressed in his classic *The Necessity for De-anglicising Ireland.* Ngugi's position on the relation of writers to their native African languages is summarized by him as follows:

"The choice of language and the use to which language is put is central to a people's definition of themselves in relation to the natural and social environment, indeed in relation to the entire universe... writers who should have been mapping paths out of that linguistic encirclement [by colonialism] of their continent also came to be defined and to define themselves in terms of the language of imperialist imposition. Even at their most radical and pro-African position in their sentiments and articulation of problems they still took it as axiomatic that the renaissance of African cultures lay in the languages of Europe."

Thiong'o referred scathingly to a 1962 African writers conference in Kampala, Uganda that excluded writers who wrote in African languages, in which questions of what African literature is or could be were discussed, while accepting that said literature had to be in English, Ngugi summarizes the basis of this phenomenon, recurrent in almost every colonial/neo-colonial contexts as follows:

"The bullet was the means of the physical subjugation. Language was the means of the spiritual subjugation."

He speaks of school, wherein he was forced to learn English and witness how English was used to sort students into a pyramidal hierarchy. No matter how clever you were, you were not allowed to continue if you couldn't use English well. At the same time, reminiscent of the Irish National School system introduced by the British Government in 1831, students were banned from, even punished for, using their own language.

Thiong'o discusses the effect of colonial imposition of a foreign language on children. By so doing, according to him, it unavoidably undervalued the child's home culture and elevated the status of the "language of the colonizer", in his case: English. This divorce broke the harmony between the spoken and written language, producing the cultural alienation that created native intellectuals such as Senghor or Achebe or Banda (in Malawi) who sang the praises of the colonizer's language to the detriment of their own.

This denial of the native language is the highest proof that the linguistic suppression has accomplished its work, and explains Thiong'o's reference to that anomalous 1962 English-only African writer's conference (and, incidentally, such "anomalies" have become the norm in 21st century Ireland):

"The very fact that what common sense dictates in

the literary practice of other cultures [to write in your own spoken language] is being questioned in an African writer is a measure of how far imperialism has distorted the view of African realities. It has turned reality upside down: the abnormal is viewed as normal and the normal is viewed as abnormal...Africa even produces intellectuals who now rationalize this upside-down way of looking at Africa."

Substituting the words "Irish" for "African", has our "upside-down" way of looking at Ireland and Irish now become "normalized"? Are we living in a topsy-turvy republic where writers and intellectuals rationalize their upside-down way of looking at Ireland as being their pragmatic response to a perceived need to habituate themselves to the "new normal" of topsy-turvydom?

However, they, and many African counterparts, can also claim, with full justification, that writing in little-read or, still less, little-understood languages places little, if any, bread on the table.

AND BACK TO EUROPE

Let us now consider the following somewhat lengthy quotation that presents a highly relevant, albeit controversial in some respects, Latvian perspective on colonialism and the language question. The Latvian language—a Baltic language, along with Lithuanian—was considered by its author, Karl E. Jirgens[*], to have been

---

[*]*Language and Decolonization: A Latvian Perspective,* Karl E. Jirgens (Lituanus: Lithuanian Quarterly Journal of Arts and Sciences ,Volume 44, No.3 - Fall 1998.)

subject to a de facto marginalization by Russian while Latvia formed a part of Soviet Russia between 1940 and 1991:

"In his study on linguistic patterns, Language, Thought and Reality, noted linguist Benjamin Lee Whorf, discusses early conceptions of language which began with the Greeks and persisted to the twentieth century. He suggests that in the classical Greek period, it was believed that a thought in any given language could be grasped by all and that ideas could be readily translated from one language to another. This view persisted over the centuries and even recently it was held that a thought expressed in one language could be translated without loss of meaning into any other language.

But, Whorf demonstrated that this view of translation was flawed. He explained that a language actually shapes the world-view of a people. There is more to translation than simply finding corresponding words. One must also recognize the cultural differences, and differences in world-view that accompany each language. The conception of time, for example, can be radically different in various cultures. These differences in world-view, are also integral to the language of each people. "A change in language," argues Whorf, "can transform our appreciation of the Cosmos". If one considers the implications of Whorf's theory regarding psychic colonization, then, the Russo-Soviet agenda of eradication of the native language can also be seen as a frontal attack against a particular world-view. I contend *that it is the undermining of this world-view that has led to the psychic malaise presently evident in Latvia.*

However, a restoration of cultural identity is considerably more complex than achieving political independence.

Again, the struggle turns to matters of cultural integration, and more specifically, to language. As Foucault has repeatedly explained, language is power, and those who control the channels of discourse or language, also hold the power. The deeper meaning of this struggle becomes apparent when one overlaps Foucault's theory with Whorf's view of the connections between language and world-view. Consider the extent to which a linguistic environment shapes a culture and national world-view. To be within a linguistic environment that consists of a foreign or alien language places the individual at a decided practical disadvantage... Being outside a language stigmatizes the individual and brands them as an outsider... In relatively benevolent cultures... this stigmatization is less objectionable than it is in a situation where the dominant language is also used to exercise power and oppression over the mind-set of an entire nation. To be displaced, set apart as an "outsider" within the borders of one's own nation is demoralizing, and disheartening. One cannot throw aside the sense of oppression until one can throw aside the language of oppression. To be truly free, one must also be free within one's own language, and the world-view that language embraces.

It is clear that in spite of pressures from a newly empowered Latvian government, a majority of Russian residents have chosen to ignore citizenship language requirements. It is equally clear that an unprecedented agenda of linguistic and cultural degradation was conducted in Latvia during its fifty year occupation by the Soviet. Although Latvia was occupied by other nations in the past... none but the Soviet Union insisted on subjugating and eradicating the Latvian language. This genealogical tracing of the sustained attack against the native Latvian language by the occupying Soviet force begs a question. Why is the struggle over language so insistent?

If, as Benjamin Lee Whorf contends, one's linguistic environment can shape one's world-view, and one's identity, then the ramifications of Russification become rather apparent, and the reason for Russians resisting the re-installation of the native Latvian language becomes equally apparent.[*]

In order to continue economic domination of the region, it is highly advantageous to Moscow to maintain a psychic mode of colonization, even if the political colonization has technically come to an end with Latvia's independence at the turn of this decade. During the fifty years period of occupation, Latvians were persistently diverted from their self-identity...

---

[*]It should be mentioned here that in the middle of the last century Whorf's views fell out of favor and were criticized and rejected by academics, including the renowned linguist and political activist, Noam Chomsky, who considered language structure to primarily reflect cognitive universals rather than cultural differences. However, Whorfian ideas have experienced resurgence in more recent times. The present writer's experience as a translator, rendering Spanish and Catalan texts into Irish, and vice-versa, and Irish texts into English, inclines him towards accepting the key element of Whorf's linguistic thesis.

pressured into a loss of 'belief in their names, in their languages, in their environment, in their heritage of struggle, in their unity, in their capacities and ultimately in themselves.' In the after-shock of occupation, the Latvian psyche is highly vulnerable and malleable. It suffers from a collective lack of self-confidence or self-esteem. The former imperial power is still perceived as vital to the well-being of the nation, and the language of the occupying nation still signifies an economic and cultural potency that appears to be lacking in Latvia.

Whether this perception is accurate is beside the point. What does matter is the sense that the culture of the former empire as Other is perceived too often as being desirable to the traditional and indigenous culture of Latvia. Language lies at the heart of the matter and currently, at the heart of the heart is the besieged Latvian world-view. This heart is the arena of struggle for Latvia's self-actualization. When one considers the shaping power of language in the form of folk-songs, story-telling, poetry, and mythology, and adds to these the daily impact of street signs, billboards, advertisements, educational materials, maps, history books, newspapers, radio and television reports, then one can see the power of language in shaping and affecting the cultural psyche and world-view of a people. I contend that it is language itself, complete with its extensive and embedded cultural history that ultimately defines a people. While advances have been made in both political and economic directions, a decolonization of the mind will be slow until the Latvian language is convincingly re-established. The political, economic, and *cultural reclamation of Latvia is currently enjoying slow but steady progress. However this progress can be accelerated primarily through a re-assertion of language, and it is largely in this linguistic arena that the de-colonization of the Latvian psyche will occur."*

Compare the psychological effects of fifty years of the linguistic oppression endured by Latvia, alleged by Dr. Jirgens, to the possible enduring effects of Ireland's linguistic and political suppression that lasted almost ten times as long. Consider the matter-of-factness of the final sentence of his article with the amazement with which the proposition that, *"language is the heart of the matter"* and *"it is largely in this linguistic arena that the decolonization of the Irish psyche will occur"* would be greeted in present-day Ireland!

Language loss and the subjection of the nation to intense and brutal colonization, where understood at all, would not be considered by most Irish citizens to have any contemporary impact whatsoever. In a manner reminiscent of survivors of other human disasters, most of such "unpleasantness" seems to have been excised, in an exercise of a seeming mental hygiene, from the minds of the latter. Thus, they live, arguably, in the words of a friend of mine, in *"a state of collective historical amnesia"*. So, as far as the generality of Irish citizenry is concerned the concept of decolonization can only be totally irrelevant to its present cultural concerns!

Bearing this in mind, let us now summarize those historical and contemporary developments that culminated in the formation of the affective and intellectual bases of contemporary Irishness. Briefly, the hypothesis to be developed is that the SCIS (Super-Colonized Irish Syndrome) evolved during three successive major colonizations of the Irish mind is central to this essay.

Innate to this hypothesis is the idea that the cultural and psychological effects of each of these historic interventions were internalized by significant sections of the Irish population. The latter reacted to these by evolving affective and cognitive complexes that interact mutually to give contemporary Irish thought and behavior its distinctive cast in a European context. However, many SCIS-like symptoms may also be displayed by other European ethnic groups whose cultures underwent a similar destruction (e.g. Bretons, Scottish Gaels, Sami, et al.).

Also innate to this hypothesis, based on evidence to be discussed later, is the proposition that SCIS may have a significant biological basis. This will account, at least partly, for the observation that the culture developed by colonized subjects is transmissible from generation to generation, so that its symptoms may be exhibited by generations far removed from the original trauma of colonization.

SCIS has more in common with the similar, if not identical, complexes that afflict other peoples who were brutally colonized rather than with the world outlook and psychology of those other nations— such as some of our present European partners— who, being the more ruthless perpetrators of organized violence, saddled themselves with the God-given colonizing mission of "civilizing" various recalcitrant indigenous peoples around the globe!

Thence, quotations from the writings of some Third World thinkers involved in anticolonial struggle will punctuate this essay and underline the common trauma of all colonized indigenous peoples, including the Irish, who have passed through the wringer of "civilizing" colonizations.

THE FIRST COLONIZATION OF
THE IRISH MIND

THE ROOTS OF SCIS

The First Colonization of the Irish Mind proceeded, in earnest, after the defeat of the Irish-Spanish force by English forces in Kinsale in 1601 that was the beginning of the end of Gaelic hegemony in any part of Ireland. It initiated a further strengthening of England's military, political and cultural hegemony throughout the island during the 17th and 18th centuries.

Replacement of the previously dominant Gaelic civil order and culture by its English equivalent and the futility of serious resistance to England's superior organized armed might, led gradually to a sullen, acceptance of the new status quo—punctuated by uprisings against the colonizing power—by most of the Gaelic Irish. The implications of the brutal enforcement of English law and custom were to be linguistically, culturally and psychologically both far-reaching and long-lasting.

In the latter regard, the Irish were by no means exceptional. For, the colonization process, no matter where it occurs, entails an almost inevitable algorhythmic progression from the condition of free culturally independent agents to that of super-colonized subjects reduced to economic and cultural dependence on their colonial masters.

THE BIRTH OF PADDY

Ireland was the original colonized nation, and was subjected to a near-genocidal conquest centuries before the Holocaust. It was where the policies of the British Empire were road-tested for use in India and Africa, and where a subject population stripped of property and political rights was then blamed for its own poverty. The island's native people, despite their white skin, were viewed as savage and barbaric because they did not speak English, practiced an alien religion and hewed to unfamiliar cultural customs. During the Great Famine of the 1840s, which produced a huge wave of Irish emigration to America, the Irish poor were starved to death or driven off their own land by the millions. Yes, the potato—a plant imported from South America by the British—had been ruined by blight, but the famine itself was avoidable. Its true cause was not the black fungus that turned the prátaí to inedible mush, but a pseudo-Darwinian, proto-Milton Friedman free market ideology, insisted upon at a time when Ireland as a whole was a net exporter of food.

Andrew O'Hehir
How did my fellow Irish-Americans get so disgusting? Salon Saturday, March 15, 2014.

Left without any serious hope of redressing their woes, most colonized subjects become resigned to their fate, exhibiting the very symptoms of their condition, as related to them by the colonizer.

The psychological consequences of living under the conditions of repressive colonial regimes were spelled out in detail by such seminal investigators of colonial cultural dynamics as Albert Memmi (b. Tunisia 1920), writer and author of a classic, *The Colonizer and the Colonized*, Franz Fanon (b. Martinique 1925), psychiatrist and revolutionary associated with the struggle for Algerian independence, author of *Wretched of the Earth* and *Black Skins, White Masks*, and Ngũgĩ wa Thiong'o, author of *Decolonizing the Mind*.

The analyses of these writers highlight the strong cultural ambivalence of the colonized subject: a deep sense of shame at his origins and being among the defeated co-existing, paradoxically, with nostalgia for his past, his own culture and language.

The colonial cultural order grows out of the colonizer's racist, hierarchical conception of human capacities. Self-fulfilling colonial mythologies are created: charged with laziness by the colonizer, the colonized receives no reward for work done and, ergo, becomes unwilling to work, which is to say, congenitally lazy. The North American colonizer feeds indigenous Americans rotgut whiskey, so many of the latter become drunkards. Albert Memmi considered the basic function of such mythologies in the colonizer's economic order:

"Let us imagine... the oft-cited trait of laziness. It seems to receive unanimous approval from Liberia to Laos, via the Maghreb. It is easy to see to what extent this description is useful It occupies an important place

in the dialectics exalting the colonizer and humbling the colonized. Furthermore, it is economically fruitful.

Nothing could better justify the colonizer's privileged position than his industry, and nothing could better justify the colonized's destitution than his indolence. The mythical portrait of the colonized therefore includes an unbelievable laziness and that of the colonizer, a virtuous taste for action. At the same time the colonizer suggests that employing the colonized is not very profitable, thereby authorizing his unreasonable wages."

The key role of sweated Irish labor over three centuries in the building and maintenance of Britain's agricultural and transport infrastructures, as well as being the backbone of its construction industry in recent times, is relevant in that context. Likewise, the role of cheap Irish labor in the construction of canals and railroads in the U.S.A, logging in Tasmania, and earlier, in the 17th Century Cromwellian epoch, as indentured servants, effectively slave labor, in the Barbadoes and West Indies.

The Irish colonized subject understood from his English master that he was of a lower order of being, gormless but sly, humorous and sometimes charming. The quintessential Paddy was scatterbrained and childlike, thus inherently incapable of governing himself or his own kind. Thus, he needed the benevolent guidance of the colonizer to direct his life—even when that life was the site of the shameless exploitation of his own labor power. Paddy internalized this self-demeaning myth, simultaneously displacing his preexisting Gaelic mythic self as this false consciousness, and the understanding of his true place in the overall colonial dispensation, was taking hold.

Thus, a descendant of coffin ship survivors was able to tell my wife in New York that the Great Hunger occurred because the Irish who lived on coasts, God love (and help) them, were so inefficient, lazy and shiftless that, when the potato crop failed, well, the poor unfortunate *divils*, they weren't even able to learn how to fish...

THE HOAXING OF PADDY

Memmi considered the impact of the colonizer's imaging of the colonized on the self-imaging of the latter:

"Constantly confronted with this image of himself, set forth and imposed on all institutions and in every human contact, how could the colonized help reacting to his portrait? It cannot leave him indifferent and remain a veneer which, like an insult, blows with the wind. He winds up recognizing it as one would a detested nickname which has become a familiar description. The accusation disturbs him and worries him even more because he admires and fears his powerful accuser. 'Is he not partially right?' he mutters. 'Are we not all a little guilty after all? Lazy, because we have so many idlers. Timid, because we let ourselves be oppressed.' Willfully created and spread by the colonizer, this

mythical and degrading portrait ends up by being accepted and lived with to a certain extent by the colonized. It thus acquires a certain amount of reality and contributes to the true portrait of the colonized.

This process is not unknown. It is a hoax. It is common knowledge that the ideology of a governing class is adopted in large measure by the governed classes... By agreeing to this ideology, the dominated classes practically confirm the role assigned to them. This explains, inter alia, the relative stability of societies; oppression is tolerated willy-nilly by the oppressed themselves...

Just as the colonizer is tempted to accept his part, the colonized is forced to accept being colonized."

The eventual stability of this colonizer-colonized bifurcation is one specific example of what Social Psychology defines as "status quo rationalization through the use of stereotypes". Another common example of such stereotyping in system justification is the classic Marxist bourgeoisie–proletariat divide that characterizes the capitalist social order wherever it becomes established.

Specifically, on perceiving threats to the prevailing system, people will incline towards justifying the status quo by utilizing stereotypes. Perceiving their group to be a high-status in-group (e.g. colonizers, English, bourgeoisie) they select stereotypes favorable to their group, and less so toward a low-status outgroup (e.g. the colonized, Irish, Irish speakers, workers). On the other hand, if people perceive their groups to be low-status, they adopt less favorable stereotypes of their own group, and more favorable stereotypes of high-status outgroups.

Social psychology theorists hold that low-status-outgroup members (such as colonized subjects, workers, et al.) provide explanations, no matter how weak (e.g. "There is no alternative"), to rationalize unequal group status differences. They tend to associate positive characteristics (favorable stereotypes) with high-status ingroup members (colonizers, bosses) and may lead fellow low-status group members to have more positive feelings about their low status. Alternatively, some may seek to elevate their status by attempting to conform to the favorable stereotype of the high-status group.

Thus, accompanying the colonial status quo, Memmi—analyzing, like Fanon, colonization in a North African context in his *The Colonizer and the Colonized*—identifies the strong propensity of the colonized subject to imitate the language and manners of his colonial master. The colonized strives to be like the colonizer, to become him, to be "white" in his tastes and manners. He internalizes the colonizers' world outlook, as far as such is possible for a North African. To please the colonizer, he conforms to stereotypes devised for him by the latter.

As expressed by Paolo Freire (b. 1921), the Brazilian educator and cultural commentator:

"For cultural invasion to succeed, it is essential that those invaded become convinced of their intrinsic

inferiority… The more the invasion is accentuated and those invaded are alienated from the spirit of their own culture and from themselves, the latter want to be like the invaders: to walk like them, talk like them."

The social psychology concept of system-justification enables us to understand both the contradiction inherent to colonizer-colonized relationships along with the stability of the latter. Likewise, that of the capitalist order in spite of its manifestly unequal distribution of socially created wealth. And why colonized subjects kowtow to the demeaning demands of the colonizer. The concept refers to psychological processes contributing to preservation of existing social arrangements even at the expense of personal and group interests. It consists of defense of the status quo, at all costs.

So, the notion of system-justification accounts for previously unexplained phenomena, most notably the promulgation by disadvantaged individuals and groups of negative stereotypes of themselves, and the consensual nature of stereotypic beliefs despite differences in social relations within and between social/ethnic groups.

There is ample evidence for the operation of such principles within past and present Irish social/cultural landscapes.

PADDY TALKS DACENT

To end colonization, the colonized must discover that the colonizer's myth or stereotype concerning himself, and that he has internalized, is just that: a myth, a hoax, as Memmi suggests.

The system-justification principle suggests to us, however, that the colonized is more inclined to hang on to cherish this "hoax" than to disembarrass himself of it. He will defend an unjust and exploitative status quo in which he may be the lowest of the low in the pecking order because he is, at least, included and can survive as long as he obeys the rules of that pecking order.

Fanon suggests that the profound depersonalization involved in internalization of the colonizer's "hoax" is a major factor in the development of the many mental disorders of the colonized identified by him. This idea was to be explored in depth by later students of the psychopathology of colonialism.

From Fanon's perspective, true national liberation must involve two essential phases: firstly, forcing the colonizer to withdraw and then, secondly, the destruction by the colonized subject of the colonizer's myth within him. This was held by him to apply to all situations in which the paradigmatic colonizer-colonized relationship, as described by him, developed.

Fanon also noted that the low-status outgroup mentality of the colonized subject can survive the formal independence of former colonies. He envisaged political liberation, then, as being merely the initial phase of national liberation. Cultural decolonization had to follow to complete the liberation process.

Colonialism put down older and stronger roots in Ireland than in Fanon's Algeria, however. Therefore, did it really induce, to an irreversible degree, that profound psychological, cultural and, possibly, biological changes (as we will see later) that colonial regimes almost inevitably produce in their subject populations?

An example from contemporary Ireland of the thoroughness with which the colonizer's myth of the colonized was internalized by the latter is afforded by the patronizing or hostile reaction to native Irish Gaelic by "polite" Irish society (i.e. affluent in-group sections that fully internalized, and now perpetuate, the departed colonizer's mythic Irishry). Thus, the Irish language can be described variously as charming though outdated, and folkloric by such thoroughly acculturated colonized subjects, to being embarrassing, foreign, a throw-back to a thankfully forgotten past, a useless "bog-language".

Douglas Hyde noted a similar tendency over a century ago, according to his *The Necessity for De-anglicising Ireland*, the original "bible" of Irish language revivalism. Also, according to Hyde, the shamefaced self-negation of native Irish speakers even denying that they could speak Irish existed in his time.

That phenomenon is still encountered. A well-known Belfast language activist likes to tell the story of how he stopped his car in the heart of the Donegal *Gaeltacht* to ask the way, in Irish, of a local inhabitant:

"There is no Irish at me," says the native.
"There's no bloody English at you either," says the Belfastman, as he takes his foot off the brake...

ENGLAND'S CULTURAL POLICY IN IRELAND?

Extirpation of the Irish language was always a key aim of English cultural policy in its Irish colony. Strictures banning the use of Irish, the most obvious and visible manifestation of national and cultural difference—and thence a potential for resistance to the colonial diktat—were enforced in certain places and at certain times. Anglicization of the Irish population was seen to be the surest way to ensure the permanent acceptance by the "Wild Irish" of English rule and customs and, thus, of their condition as colonized subjects within the then Anglosphere economic order.

Under the Statutes of Kilkenny, 1366, written originally in French, the then administrative language of England, use of Irish language and dress was proscribed. Outside The Pale, Dublin and surrounding areas, this ruling was largely ignored. Contemporary records show that even within the city boundaries of Dublin at that time, the Irish language was in common use. With the 16th century Tudor reconquest of most of Ireland, however, a more vigorous attempt to replace Gaelic with English was initiated.

An English colonizer of that period, the poet Edmund Spenser (b. 1552), author of *The Faerie Queene*, wrote a treatise, *A View of the Present State of Ireland*, in which he advocated the destruction of Irish language and culture, arguing that if the language were Irish, so—inevitably—would be the heart the of the Irish-speaker. He intuited shrewdly, in a pre-Whorfian insight, that to obliterate a language was to obliterate a world view:

"The words are the image of the mynde, the mynde must needs be affected with the words: So that the speech beinge Irishe, the harte must needs be Irishe, for out of the aboundance of the harte the tongue speaketh."

Thence, according to Spenser, if the Irish could be forced to adopt English, they would come to accept in large measure the world-view enshrined by that language, including the definition of their own place and nature within that world-view.

Spenser's stance was in line with general English linguistic/cultural policy in territories of ruled by the English crown. Thus, almost 300 years later, what Matthew Arnold (b. 1822 - d. 1888), a great proponent of English cultural policy throughout England's dominions, wrote about Welsh, was fully coherent with Spenser's stance regarding Irish. The fate proposed by the former for Welsh, a sister Celtic language of Irish, philologically speaking, and regarded by Arnold as being "the curse of Wales", could just as well have been proposed for the Gaelics of Ireland, Scotland and the Isle of Man along with the little that remained of the Cornish of Cornwall. He wrote:

"The fusion of all the inhabitants of these islands into one homogeneous, English-speaking whole, the breaking down of barriers between us, the swallowing

up of separate provincial nationalities, is a consummation to which the natural course of things irresistibly tends; it is a necessity of what is called modern civilisation, and modern civilisation is a real, legitimate force; the change must come, and its accomplishment is a mere affair of time. The sooner the Welsh language disappears as an instrument of the practical, political, social life of Wales, the better; the better for England, the better for Wales itself. Traders and tourists do excellent service by pushing the English wedge farther and farther into the heart of the principality; Ministers of Education, by hammering it harder and harder into the elementary schools. Nor, perhaps, can one have much sympathy with the literary cultivation of Welsh as an instrument of living literature; and in this respect Eisteddfods encourage, I think, a fantastic and mischief-working delusion. For all modern purposes, I repeat, let us all as soon as possible be one people; let the Welshman speak English, and, if he is an author, let him write English."

Such inflexibility characterizes linguistic imperialists everywhere. The French republican is scandalized by spoken Breton in Brittany, German in Alsace, Catalan in Perpignan, Basque in Bayonne and Biarritz, or even Antillean Creole and North American and Quebecois French, seen by him as being quaint. The rabid Spanish centralist abhors peninsular Catalan, Basque and Galician, just as his *Conquistador* forebears abhorred the indigenous languages of the Antilles and the Americas.

Zealots of the "English Only" movement in the

U.S.A. are so many Canutes or Caligulas fighting the rising tide of Spanish, now establishing a firm foothold in Uncle Sam's own fiefdom. Successive waves of Hispanic immigration, arriving from the Caribbean, Mexico, Central and South America, are boosting the country's native-born Spanish-speaking population, located mainly in the southwestern U.S.A., where the presence of Spanish long predates that of English.

Ironically, almost a century and a half after Arnold, such hard-core English imperialist sentiments are expressed by many present-day Irish. Never having challenged, the colonizer's myth regarding Irish cultural inferiority, they tend to reference London, rather than Dublin, as their cultural capital. For such end-products of centuries of cultural brainwashing, Anglosphere literature, art and civilization are the apex of mankind's cultural achievement.

Within the world-view of such products of England's centuries-long cultural strategy in Ireland, Irish Gaelic culture and literature figure as embarrassing and unwelcome interlopers on the contemporary Irish cultural scene: throwbacks to a primitive, pre-modern, phase of Ireland's painful historical development through bloodstained centuries whose reality and contemporary significance such "cosmopolitan" anglophiles studiously ignore.

Their attitude is celebrated, unsurprisingly, by the gurus of Ireland's supercolonized media as evidence that the Irish, as a people, have, at last, achieved that level of "maturity" required to qualify for inclusion in the list of European civilized nations.

Thus, contributions in Irish to cultural debate in present-day Ireland are largely ignored by the gatekeepers of the country's national mass-media. This observation even applies to Irish-language media that, ensconced in their sense of cultural inferiority, adjudge such to be of little worth. Major Irish-language literary figures, Ó Cadhain, Ó Direáin, Ó Riordáin, et al., seldom figure in iconographies of 20th century Irish literature.

These omissions cause even Irish speakers themselves to doubt the worth of contributions, literary or otherwise, and of which they are increasingly unlikely to be even aware, in Irish. Thus, a totally unjustified sense of the inevitable inferiority of Irish-language contributions to the national cultural output is continuously fortified.

Having the same historical roots as the loss of Irish itself, this anachronistic colonial-subject shamefacedness, the most tell-tale symptom of SCIS, has undermined every attempt to date to place the revival of Irish on a firm footing.

THE EBBTIDE OF IRISH

"The colonized... will never have anything but their native tongue; that is, a tongue which is neither written nor read, permitting only uncertain and poor oral development.

Granted, small groups of academics persist in developing the language of their people, perpetuating it through scholarly pursuits into the splendors of the past. But its subtle forms bear no relationship to everyday life, or was used across the counters of government offices, or directed the postal service; but this is not the case. The entire bureaucracy, the entire court system, all industry hears and uses the colonizer's language...

Furthermore, the colonized's mother tongue... is precisely the one that is least valued. It has no stature in the country or in the concert of peoples. If he wants to obtain a job, make a place for himself, exist in the community and in the world, he must first bow to the language of his masters. In the linguistic conflict within the colonized, his mother tongue is that which is crushed. He himself sets about discarding this this infirm language, hiding it from the sight of strangers."

Albert Memmi.

The negative attitude of most Irish towards their ancestral language has a history. On the cusp of the 18th and 19th centuries, thanks to the colonizer's contempt (with some exceptions) for the culture and language of the Irish colonized subject, both the Gaelic majority and the burgeoning post-Gaelic minority in Ireland were starting to see this language through the colonizer's eyes. Assimilation of these colonizer's attitudes to Irish popular ideology strengthened as the tide of Irish ebbed.

Needless to say, such a negative appreciation of historic Irish ethnicity, surviving the achievement of partial independence in 1921, was bound to have a powerful demotivating influence on the learning of Irish. This factor is tremendously resilient and that has survived, as strong as ever, up to our present day in 21st century Ireland. That is, more than a century after Hyde founded the Gaelic

League in Dublin in 1893, in his heroic, though ultimately vain, attempt to stem the advancing floodtide of linguistic and cultural Anglicization.

However, let us now backtrack a little to trace some of the key moments that led to the deep rootedness of high-group (colonizer's) cultural values in the collective Irish psyche.

A profound sense of shame and cultural inferiority developed in the 18th and 19th centuries among the Irish-speakers of England's Irish colony. With the spread of bilingualism, it gradually sapped the popular will to continue speaking Irish. The language was gradually abandoned, sometimes reluctantly, occasionally with a palpable sense of relief, if patterns of the Irish to English language shift observable the 21st century *Gaeltacht* are a reliable guide. This relief is often tinged with guilt feelings, "like abandoning your mother", as one such latter-day linguistic "convert" described to me her feelings on abandoning Irish!

The so-called Catholic "Liberator" of the early 19th century, Daniel O'Connell, himself a native Irish speaker, equated Irish identity almost exclusively with profession of the Catholic religion. He explained his rejection of Irish as follows:

"I am sufficiently utilitarian not to regret its the Irish language's) abandonment. A diversity of tongues is not (of) benefit; it was imposed on mankind as a curse at the building of Babel. It would be of vast advantage to mankind if all the inhabitants of the earth spoke the same language. Therefore, though

the Irish language is connected with many recollections that twine around the hearts of Irishmen, yet the superior utility of the English tongue as the medium of all modern communication, is so great that I can witness without a sigh the gradual disuse of Irish.*"*

O'Connell, looked upon as a national liberator by his fellow countrymen, demonstrated this attitude towards Irish by speaking only English, even in areas where Irish was the only language understood by most of his listeners. The intended destination of his statements from electoral campaign platforms may well have been the front pages of English newspapers. Nevertheless, translators conveyed O'Connell's not so subliminal and highly influential anti-Gaelic sentiment to the crowds listening to the "Liberator's" message of Catholic Emancipation. Such sentiments still inform the cultural stance of many of O'Connell's "utilitarian" successors across the political divides of contemporary Ireland.

However, it must be noted out that English had become the language of Irish emancipatory discourse, of Irish nationalism itself, since the end of the 17th century. Individual revolutionary leaders, Patrick Pearse being the prime example, wished for Irish and English to be on the same official footing in a

---

*Quoted in Patrick Rafroidi, *Irish Literature in English, The Romantic Period*, Gerrards Cross 1980, Vol. 2, p.xxi, citing Houston, ed.

notionally independent Ireland. (Significantly, his main political writings were in English while his literary contributions were almost all in Irish.)

However, the attempted actualization of such an ambitious linguistic aim was always destined to founder on the rock of strong colonial anti-Irish-language sentiment that seems to have become deeply internalized by the colonized Irish masses during and after abandoning their ancestral language.

So, thanks in large measure to this developing innate cultural/linguistic shamefacedness, along with the opposition of its political leadership and clergy to the native language, Irish, by the mid-19th century, was reduced to being a minority language in an Ireland in which it had been almost the sole language for over 2000 years.

Máirtín Ó Cadhain, the greatest writer to date of Irish Gaelic fiction—and one of Ireland's greatest ever—cited 1820 in his *Destined to Pass*, as being, in his view, the year that marked the turning point that presaged the end of that dominance.

Thereafter the sway of Irish was rapidly corroded, starting in the east of the country, with the gradual encroachment westwards of English. Massive 19th emigration from Ireland, due to famine, the threat of famine and rural poverty, the consequences of the implementation of English colonial economic policies in Ireland, was mainly to English-speaking countries. This reality gave a powerful economic stimulus to the anglicizing bent of the potential emigrant, derived from his religious and lay leaders.

(The emigration factor still has a strong contemporary

relevance in Ireland. Subservience to the dictates of the ECB, WB and IMF, the "men in black" of the "Troika" by compliant Irish Governments led to deteriorated social and economic conditions that led, in their turn, to the emigration of over 200,000 of young people between 2009 and 2014.)

Likewise, the fact that primary education, instituted in 1831 by the British Government was, at the behest of parents and their clergy, delivered through English only. Previous to 1831, "hedge schools", clandestine centers of learning organized in some districts by the people themselves, had been agents for the dissemination of English[*]. However, the national schools—being much more systematically organized, and on a national basis, were a much more effective instrument for delivering that effective linguistic Anglicization of almost an entire people desired by government and ecclesiastical authorities alike as well as by the overwhelming majority of parents.

Thus, due to the confluence of all of these influences, by the end of the 19th century, Irish was a minority language, spoken by approximately 20% of the population. It is now spoken by a putative miniscule 0.02%.

---

[*]Ironically, in some nationalist readings of Irish history, the same anglicising hedge schools often became transmogrified into centers for the preservation and dissemination of traditional Irish Gaelic culture.

Irish speakers who are refused Irish Government services to which they are legally entitled become painfully aware that imperial cultural policies that led to the marginalization of Irish are alive and well in post-Gaelic Ireland.

Implementation of such policies brought about the resignation in 2014 of Seán Ó Cuirreáin, the Irish State's first Irish language rights Commissioner, due to frustration at his inability to impel government departments to fulfil their legal obligations to Irish-speaking users of their services. The over-riding linguistic imperative of the Irish State apparatus is obvious: English is compulsory for all; Irish is only an optional extra.

This failure to respect the constitutional right of a linguistic minority of citizens whose sense of identity is inextricably bound to the Irish language further evidences the purely tokenistic role of the Irish language in Irish public administration.

The reluctance of the Irish state bureaucracy to meet its responsibilities to Irish–speaking citizens is no recent development. Details of the growth of such antidemocratic attitudes and decisions are recounted in Colmán Ó hUallacháin's *The Irish and Irish*, a sociolinguistic analysis of the relation between the Irish and their hereditary language since the State's foundation. More recently (2014) the gradual State withdrawal from commitment to the living language was described in detail by leading sociolinguist, Conchúr Ó Giollagáin.

Thence, the decision of Ó Cuirreáin to resign his Language Commissioner post is, arguably, the definitive statement regarding the present, and future, willingness of the Irish State to provide services for its Irish-speaking citizens.

Widespread popular indifference, often masking a latent popular resentment towards Irish, even in some official *Gaeltacht* areas, ensures that the state machine is most unlikely to come under popular pressure from below to change the circumstances that brought about Ó Cuirreáin's resignation.

Still, in spite of official indifference or outright hostility, a small minority of citizens outside the *Gaeltacht* still cherishes and speaks some Irish, often believing that such a practice defines their Irishness. Those who speak it as a first language constitute a much smaller and shrinking minority.

However, electing to be being Irish-speaking in a country whose almost sole medium of communication is English, and in which the rights of users of the State's first official language are often denied, comes with a price. It is to doom oneself all too often to perpetual frustration.

The reality is that Irish-speakers, who insist on their constitutional right to deal through Irish with the State apparatus, for example, are all too often regarded as cranks, second-class citizens and just a plain bloody nuisance.

To smooth over this denial of what should be recognized in practice as a basic democratic right, Government spokespersons intone, sporadically, a threadbare mantra to the effect that the State stays committed to the rights of Irish speakers and to the revival of the Irish language etc., etc.

"Official" revivalists perpetuate this blatant untruth, papering over the catastrophic decline of Irish in the *Gaeltacht* with fanciful interpretations of census data that indicate a corresponding surge in the Irish-speaking population outside the *Gaeltacht*.

Irrespective of such almost worthless "data" and dubious vox-pop survey results, objective real-life observation establishes that most Irish people are indifferent towards the Irish language or guardedly, if not openly, hostile towards it.

Hence, State indifference to the rights of Irish speakers is hardly surprising, given that Irish Free State and subsequent linguistic policy, mainly implemented through the State educational system, never breached popular resistance to readopting Irish as the nation's main spoken language.

Thence, the present Irish State never comes under significant popular pressure to honor its obligations to Irish-speaking citizens.

The fact that the real status of the Irish language in Ireland is purely symbolic, ceremonial and folkloric was always, and still is, well understood by the population at large, Irish-speaking *Gaeltacht* inhabitants included.

Thus, the imperial aim of the Anglicization of Ireland is approaching full realization, ironically under the auspices of an Irish State whose first official language is Irish.

WHENCE THE IDEOLOGY OF TOKENISM?

Why, then, given the popular rejection of spoken Irish, does the Irish State and a majority of its citizens "cherish" Irish as a symbol of Irishness?

Could it be that the mere existence of the language buttresses the claim—central to Irish nationalist ideology—that we Irish are a separate nationality, being in an unbroken line of descent from the people of the historic Irish nation? Thereby, it can be asserted that we remain a people completely distinct from those of our British neighbors, in spite of the glaringly obvious fact that contemporary Ireland shares a more or less common British Isles culture?

Our right to be an independent administrative entity, separate from that of Britain, can thus be asserted on the basis of ethnic difference evidenced by the continued, albeit greatly attenuated, presence of Irish.

Also, by espousing the Irish language as a national symbol, Anglophone post-Gaelic Ireland is able to imagine itself to be in fanciful continuity with an ersatz pre-colonized historic Irish nation, an 18th and 19th century romantic Irish Literary Revival invention, popularized by Anglophone nationalists and peopled by Celtic heroes "taller than Roman spears".

Some prominent Irish Literary Renaissance figures, such as William Butler Yeats, even figured that a distinctive Anglophone Irish national culture could be constructed from such imaginings, as farfetched as that notion now seems in the cold light of 2014.

Irish linguistic ambivalence was resolved, with the founding of the Irish State, by making Irish the latter's first official language.

The symbolism underlying this gesture was made obvious by the State's egregious disinterest in the survival of the spoken language. While official spokespersons were claiming that the State aimed to Gaelicize popular speech, the then extensive areas where Irish was actually spoken, the *Gaeltachtaí*, mainly impoverished districts on the western seaboard, were allowed to be devastated by emigration. Thus, the scene for the eventual final collapse of the Irish-speaking communities, now at hand, was already set by a State machine whose resistance to serious nation-wide Gaelicization was clear from its very beginnings.

After the departure of Ireland's colonial administrators, the business of the modern sectors of Free State society, legislature, administration, law, medicine, science and technology, culture, etc., continued to be conducted, with the very occasional exception, through English. The main responsibility for the "revival" of Irish was delegated almost exclusively, to the nation's schools.

By relegating of Irish to the status of national symbol, obligatory school subject and pastime language the State was able to claim the sincerity of its commitment to Irish. At the same time it was enabled to wash its hands of any real responsibility for taking serious steps to ensure the continuity of the language in areas where it was still spoken and for its integration into those modern sectors over which the State had control.

The reality of Irish-language tokenism was revealed once again by a Eurocrat offer, made during negotiations in 1970-1 for Ireland's entry into the

Common Market, to grant full European official status to Irish. This offer was refused by the Irish negotiators, who, in a display of neo-colonial subservience to high-status group cultural values, denied the first official language of their own State full official EEC status.

The more recent and successful battle to secure full official EU status for Irish was—according to reliable sources—conducted, initially at least, in the teeth of official hostility to the idea by Irish administration apparatchiks in Dublin and Brussels.

However, from the 1970s onwards, the State administration saw clearly that its linguistic remit was do the minimum needed to conserve Irish as a pastime or "heritage" language in a uniformly Anglophone republic. Thus, its role went from that of "revivalist to undertaker" in the words of Conchúr Ó Giollagáin.

HEAR NO EVIL, SEE NO EVIL!

Given the near universality of super-colonized thinking in Ireland, the misfortunes of the Irish language—even the colonization of Ireland itself—scarcely figures in dominant Irish history narratives nor in secondary school history texts that present disparate fragments of such narratives. Indeed, the study of Irish history—or any history whatsoever—is no longer (2014) compulsory at any level in the Irish secondary level school system.

Thence, the relation of language loss to the cultural colonization of Ireland is totally unknown to the vast majority of Irish people who have but the vaguest idea, if any at all, that such—with its accompanying and continuing psychological trauma—ever occurred. The colonizer's ultimate linguistic/cultural ideal, that of Spenser and Arnold, is just about to be realized, ironically, under the auspices of a notionally independent Irish state.

The latter contention is confirmed by the lucubrations of many contemporary Irish intellectuals who aver that linguistic Anglicization, albeit sometimes admittedly painful at the time, was, in the end, a beneficial, crucial and necessary step towards the root and branch modernization of the Post-Gaelic Ireland that we now know.

Having fully internalized the colonizer's stereotype of themselves, and annihilated their precolonized identity, how could such supercolonized individuals be even expected to consider—except in wayward acts of imaginative romantic indulgence—the possibility of renovating a self that no longer exists?

IRELAND'S HALF-REVOLUTION

English cultural/linguistic policy in Ireland was spectacularly successful. Monolingual Gaelic-speaking Ireland was turned into an overwhelmingly and largely English-speaking country. This crushing cultural defeat is celebrated as a necessary rubric of modernization, by many—probably a majority of—Irish cultural/historical commentators. They see themselves as a fully-integrated members of a world-wide Anglophone community. A downside of this defeat, as expressed in the following editorial preface to *The Hegemony of English*, is seldom considered by them:

"It is most naïve to think that the uncritical acquisition of English will always be a great benefit. What is often left unexamined, even within the academy, is how the learning of English, a dominant language, imposes upon the subordinate speakers a feeling of subordination, as their life experience, history, and language are ignored, if not sacrificed. One can safely say that English today represents a tool, par excellence, for cultural invasion, with its monopoly of the internet, international commerce, the dissemination of celluloid culture, and its role in the Disneyfication of world cultures."

Another important effect of the virtual absence of Irish is the absence of a linguistic filter, through which incoming information would automatically conform to native criteria, was described as follows by Máirín Nic Eoin:

"In the context of the globalization of English, we would lose the ability to negotiate our own terms between the local and the global; instead of being able to accommodate the global and adapt the local, we would be in danger of becoming truly provincial, mimicking the most dominant forms of Anglophone culture."

And so it has come to pass in Ireland. As a casual

inspection of Ireland's print and electronic media clearly indicates, the widespread mimicking of Anglophone culture, attitudes and ideology clearly defines the country's position as being very much a subaltern partner in the global Anglophone enterprise.

The First Colonization of the Irish Mind, integrated the Irish people into the wider Anglosphere. They bring with them their own distinctive English-language culture, a regional British variant, colored slightly by Hollywood (*The Quiet Man, Going My Way, Darby O'Gill and the Little People,* etc.) and the Irish-American diaspora (e.g. the *Galway Bay* of Bing Crosby, the mimicking of American Saint Patrick's Day parades, drum majorettes, green beer and coffee, Black Friday sales, the resurrection of the leprechaun, the logo of Boston Celtics basketball team, etc.)

By fighting for its political freedom as an independent republic, the southern part of an Ireland, truncated by Partition, gained a limited independence from England. However, armed struggle to establish national independence is only the beginning of genuine revolution.

According to Franz Fanon, the critical decolonizing moment, the demolition of the colonizer's image of the colonized in the mind of the latter, is the result of a process that must be prosecuted on the heels of gaining political independence. Only in this way, could the initial military/political victory of the colonized proceed to full liberation.

Albert Memmi understood that this second phase of national liberation was both the most critical and by far the most difficult one:

"To go all the way with his (the colonized's) revolt...He will forego the use of the colonizer's language, even if all the locks of the country turn with that key; he will change the signs and highway markings, even if he is the first to be inconvenienced."

Such cultural decolonization, in Fanon's and Memmi's terms, never happened in Ireland. Signs and highway marking remained only superficially "touched". Thence, full national liberation and cultural realization as a people, in such terms, was destined to lie beyond the grasp of the Irish people. Defeat was snatched by them, unwittingly, from the jaws of victory.

IRELAND HEAVED
AND BROUGHT FORTH -- A NEO-COLONY

Writing in the context of the Filipino cultural struggle, Geraldo Davila drew attention to a cultural/political situation generated by prosecution of the colonizer's campaign to extirpate the ancestral languages, and associated cultures, of the colonized.

"Culturally, colonialism has adopted a negation to the (native culture's) symbolic systems (including the native language)forgetting or undervaluing them even when they manifest themselves in action. This way, the eradication of the past and the idealization of the *desire to relive the cultural heritage of colonial societies constitute a situation and a system of ideas which, along with other elements, situate the colonial society as a class."*

The republican tricolor may have flown over Dublin Castle in 1922, but the Irish Free State remained tied by its economic and cultural apron strings to the coat-tails of its former colonial master. Indigenous decolonization however is no mere physical accommodation to the physical departure of the colonizer nor to the neo-colonial administrative apparatus he leaves after him.

Franz Fanon taught that it must incorporate the understanding that survival of the psychological bondage of colonialism is inevitable unless defeated by determination to fight and overcome the constraints such bondage imposes on the free development of those whose necks may still yearn, consciously or subconsciously, for the colonist's yoke.

Such revolutionary consciousness never grew in the new Irish Free State, nor afterwards, to successfully subvert the emerging neo-colonized Irish civic, religious, economic, linguistic and cultural order. Workers failed to benefit materially from the results of independence. Class consciousness, germinating in the crucible of revolutionary struggle, was crushed by the hegemony of the post-Civil War counter revolutionary bourgeoisie, in cahoots with the Catholic Church. Prerevolutionary hopes that the new Ireland would be both Gaelic and intellectually free were lost in the "carnival of reaction" that characterized the polity of the new Irish state.

Unsurprisingly, given the unpromising beginnings of a nominally free 26-county Irish State, such a revolutionary consciousness is still barely discernible in the Ireland of today. Also, the vast majority of Irish people remain totally unaware that their ancestors were colonized (and what that might have entailed), let alone never decolonized. Their country now being recognized internationally as an independent state, how can they feel the slightest need to extract themselves from a psychological bondage of which they themselves are not even aware?

So, constrained by the now almost invisible presence of the colonizer, full Irish independence from that most insidious foreign occupation, the psychological, was never achieved.

Other examples of an analogous state of affairs could be the settler societies of Canada, the United States, Australia, New Zealand, and all of Latin America. Here direct control by the British and Iberian nations respectively ceased, yet the Anglo and Iberian descendants' political, social, moral, economic, and even racial taxonomy still exists and dominates over the original indigenous populations.

But, with this crucial difference: in the postwar Ireland of the 1920s, as depicted memorably in Liam O'Flaherty's *The House of Gold*, the newborn Irish Free State evolved seamlessly into a British Catholic neo-colony managed and hegemonized by a native comprador capitalist, a gombeen, (from *gaimbín*, the Irish for profit) class that quickly adapted itself to the role of the displaced Anglo-Irish settler establishment.

And by leaving his language, through which we Irish had come to imagine ourselves and our culture, the colonial master never really left...

THE SECOND COLONIZATION OF
THE IRISH MIND

RELIGION IN THE IRISH PENAL COLONY

The Tudor conquest (or reconquest) of Ireland was named from the Tudor dynasty, which ruled England during the 16th century. Following a failed rebellion against the crown by Silken Thomas, the Earl of Kildare, in the 1530s, Henry VIII, the King of England was, by statute of the Anglo-Irish Parliament of Ireland, declared King of Ireland. His aim was to restore such central colonial authority as had been lost to the Gaelic Irish during the previous two centuries.

By conciliation and repression the conquest continued for sixty years, until 1601, when the Irish and their Spanish allies were defeated at the Battle of Kinsale, and the entire country came gradually under the nominal control of James I, exercised through his privy council at Dublin. This control was strengthened after the Flight of the Earls in 1607 and the subsequent departure of other Irish military and political leaders to the continent, thus leaving the Gaelic Irish bereft of lay leadership.

This conquest was followed by the attempted imposition of English law, language and custom on the Irish and by the extension of Anglicanism as the state religion. Thence, the Gaelic Irish found themselves caught between their almost universal acceptance of the Pope's authority and the requirements of an alternative religious allegiance demanded of them by the English monarchy.

For most of the Gael this choice was no choice. The identification of the Protestant religion with the hated oppressor *("Clann Liútair"* or "Luther's brood", as they were described sarcastically by the Gaelic poets) sealed the issue for the Irish. Henceforth, a separate Irish identity was to be founded on three pillars: those of language, culture and religion.

The importance of religion as a marker of a national identity separate from that of the English was emphasized in the writings of Irish 16th and 17th century clerical exiles on the continent—especially of those intellectuals who pushed scholarly quills in the monastic communities of Louvain/Leuven, Prague, Lisbon, etc. Thanks in large measure to their efforts, the historic Gaelic identity was rescued from total oblivion and the equation of genuine Irishness with profession of the Roman Catholic faith was established as a given, a deep-rooted sectarian sentiment that has persisted up to our own times.

Being an Irish Roman Catholic (or Presbyterian "dissenter") under the English Crown, however, meant having a grossly inferior social status to the Anglican colonizers along with being subject to a wide range of discriminatory measures regarding property holding and basic human rights, including prohibition of practice of the Roman Catholic religion. Such restrictions led to widespread resentment and occasional insurrectionary outbreaks occurred, such as that of 1641, that threatened the gains the Tudor conquest had made, particularly in the northern half of the island, where Scottish and English planters occupied the fertile lands of the dispossessed Irish.

Repression of the native Irish further intensified after the Jacobite War of William of Orange and James II, fought between 1689 and 1691, which culminated in the Siege of Limerick and the defeat of the Irish forces. The subsequent Treaty of Limerick established the hegemony of the Protestant religion in Ireland though, as a form of compensation, the rights of Catholics were supposed to be respected. However, the new rulers paid scant heed to the latter provision.

Thus, Catholics languished under the harsh so-called Penal Laws for most of the 18th century. These laws increased the privileges and power of a minority of Protestant landlords and deprived the Catholic majority as well as Protestant Dissenters, mainly located in Ulster, of fundamental civil rights.

Thence, these religious out-groups were forbidden to bear arms or own horses worth more than 5 Pounds, enter the professions or political office or have access to education unless it was under Anglican control. The Roman Catholic Hierarchy was banished. Another Penal Law was passed in 1728, under which Catholics were denied the right to vote.

Thanks to these insufferable conditions, many ambitious young Irish people emigrated to study abroad or enter the service of the various Catholic European powers, especially those of France and Spain. The armies of the latter two continental powers boasted regiments that were almost exclusively composed of Irish émigré soldiers, the so-called "Wild Geese".

POACHER TURNS GAMEKEEPER

In the course of time, the English authorities deemed it prudent to repeal many of the most objectionable Penal Laws and seek rapprochement with the Irish on the religious front. Thus, they negotiated a concordat with the Vatican which led to the foundation of Maynooth College in 1795.

The founding of this institution, although welcomed by the Gaelic Irish at the time, was destined—the Trojan Horse simile comes to mind—to deal a further severe body blow to the still predominant Gaelic language and culture.

For, from its very beginnings, clerical education in Maynooth, founded on the basis of the British-Vatican concordat, was to be exclusively through the English language. In this way, English cultural and linguistic policy in Ireland acquired a powerful native—and more than willing—collaborator, the newly empowered, but now partially anglicized, and vigorously anglicizing, Irish Roman Catholic Church.

Given the powerful influence of this church, which filled the spiritual, cultural and leadership vacuum left by the disappearance of the Gaelic civil order in the 17th century, Maynooth quickly became—hand in hand with the British civil authorities—the major anglicizing force on the island. The Roman

Catholic clergy, with notable exceptions, actively promoted English.

The use of the Irish language and its associated cultural activities were simultaneously discouraged. At the behest of Rome, the Irish Catholic Church jettisoned its own traditional hagiography. Devotional practice was "modernized" i.e. anglicized, models for new devotional practices being imported not only from the continent but also from English Roman Catholic, Anglican and other Protestant sources.

"FAITH OF OUR FATHERS"

Thus, by the mid-20th century, *Faith of Our Fathers*, the "national anthem of Catholic Ireland", was sung lustily—along with the national secular anthem, *Amhrán na bhFiann (The Soldier's Song)*—by the massed male voice choir of thousands before All-Ireland Finals in the Croke Park of my boyhood years. Few of that staunchly patriotic choir, my own father and myself included, knew that we were, in fact, singing a borrowed English Methodist hymn.

At the same time, the formerly proscribed Irish Roman Catholic Church ignored what remained of the Gaelic architectural tradition (Cormac's Chapel, the ruined Cistercian monasteries) as it embarked on its church-building program in 1829, just after Catholic Emancipation, won largely through the efforts of Daniel O'Connell, had ended the remnants of the Penal Laws. Instead, and consistent with its anglicizing policies, the architectural style selected for said program by the

Church was based initially on the British Gothic revival.

This departure, inspired mainly by the English architect, Augustus Pugin, who designed Anglican and Roman Catholic churches in both Ireland and England, greatly influenced his Irish followers. Churches of both denominations shared this architectural tradition and were frequently indistinguishable, apart from individual furnishings and details, from each other.

Such an anglicized ecclesiastical architectural culture is fully congruent with its urban surroundings. Visitors from the U.S.A. and the European Continent to Ireland have remarked to me that Dublin seems to them, architecturally, as well as culturally and linguistically, virtually indistinguishable from most North British cities.

As ecclesiastical renovation was under way, the traditional pantheon of Irish saints, Bríd Chill Dara, Caoimhín Ghleann Dá Loch, Gobnait, Neasán, Lorcán Ó Tuathail, Molaise, Colmcille, Cillian, Ciarán, Breandán et al., saints who figure in Harry Clarke's magnificent stained glass windows, with their deep roots in the Gaelic spiritual tradition, were ushered unceremoniously out through the back door

Consigned along with them to Irish Roman Catholic mainstream forgetfulness was the history of Gaelic missionary achievements: notably, the re-evangelization of much of Europe, which had returned to the "Dark Ages" following the fall of the Roman Empire, by heroic Gaelic missionaries such as Saints Columbanus, Gall, Dymphna, Fiachra, et al.

The place of the Gaelic saints in the Catholic Irish imaginary was taken by others, mainly of French and

Southern European origin, whose alleged effigies continue to grace (or is it deface ?) the interiors of many Catholic churches both in Ireland and in Ireland's "spiritual empire", as countries with significant Irish emigrant populations are, somewhat vaingloriously, called.

Traditional Gaelic prayers and devotions, such as annual "patterns" (from the Irish, *pátrún*, or "patron") at holy wells, were discouraged by the clergy, the faithful being urged to conform to devotional practices devised by the Vatican bureaucracy.

Archbishop Paul Cullen's mid-19th Century so-called "devotional revolution" was designed to impose Roman devotional orthodoxy on worshippers and so end the use of traditional devotions and prayers, often on the basis of the assertion that many of such practices were simply thinly disguised pagan rituals. Mainstream Gaelic Catholicism was thus effectively abolished in the interest of establishing a standardized Roman liturgy wherever Roman Catholicism was practiced by the Irish.

Eventually, in the 20th century, large and frequent pilgrimages to Southern European shrines, like Lourdes, Fatima and Medjugorje, were to overshadow those made to the still popular Virgin Shrine at Knock and Croagh Patrick (originally a center of pre-Christian worship), both in Co. Mayo, as well as retreats on the penitential island of Fermanagh's Lough Derg.

Holy well ceremonies in Ireland had all but disappeared by the 21st century except from some of the country's islands and western fringes, especially in places where the Gaelic tradition has not completely vanished.

Traditional devotion came to be replaced in the 20th (and 21st) centuries by the cults of Vatican-validated saints such as Saint Martin de Porres and, later, by a saint of such dubious sanctity as the Franciscan friar, Padre Pio, he of the controversial stigmata.

The effect of such clerically instigated cultural and linguistic suppression was devastating for those of the older spiritual tradition.

As the academic historian, Gearóid Ó Tuathaigh, noted:

"The abandonment of native language, to say nothing of its enforced abandonment, inevitably involves a disorienting rupture in cultural continuity at several levels; not only an alienation from landscape (place names) and inherited historical narratives and communal myths, but also a deep psychological trauma, at an individual and communal level, caused by the loss of a rich inherited matrix of wisdom and knowledge."

Declan Kiberd, in his monumental *Inventing Ireland*, doesn't hesitate to conflate Maynooth-inspired language loss into both the development of Anglophobic (and invariably Anglophone) nationalism and the desperate existential need of a deracinated and confused people for a secure ideological mooring:

"Thereafter, more and more parents who spoke only Irish to one another saw to it that English alone

was spoken by their children. A process of 'denial' soon followed. Convulsed by guilt at the enormity of what they had done, many found it most convenient to forget that there had ever been such a thing as an Irish language distinct from English. The inferiority-complex which impelled so many to give up Irish was not cured, more often exacerbated, by the gesture: and so a people in denial sought to project their own guilt elsewhere. Hence the rampant Anglophobia among many nationalists in the latter half of the nineteenth century, and the consequent writing of Irish history as a Manichean morality-tale in the first half of the twentieth. Hence, too, the over-emphasis on Catholicism as definitive of Irishness in the same period. With the native language all but gone, many found it necessary to locate the sole or central meanings of a culture in what had survived. Yet the evidence would now suggest that the Irish may be about to jettison Catholicism as unsentimentally as once they disposed of their own language."

CATOLICISME DU TYPE IRLANDAIS

This radical change in the nature of the cultural orientation of the Catholic Church in Ireland was described by An Br. M. F. Ó Conchúir, an obviously nonconforming Christian Brother, in this translation from the Irish of a short extract from his *Fothrach Folamh Gan Aird*, as introducing:

"A Victorian form of puritanism, imported spirituality and a Romanization of church structures – these merged *into a corpus of values which found expression in English, an alien language. Puzzled European theologians confronted by this impoverished mutation of a millennium of Gaelic faith-traditions could only identify it as* le Catholicisme du type irlandais."

Serious damage was inflicted on Irish language, culture and historic identity by this *Catholicisme du type irlandais*, especially when conflated to the negative psychological effects of the First Colonization. The world has been horrorized in recent times by the perverted fruits of the life-denying puritanism and sexual repression that this Jansenistic variant of Roman Catholicism propagated in Ireland by Maynooth-trained clergy.

However, the significant contribution of the First Colonization of the Irish Mind, and the chronic psychological turmoil of swathes of the Irish population caused by brutal oppression and a radical break with native culture, cannot be discounted as being yet another contributing factor to the appearance of said "perverted fruits".

Whence the burgeoning power of the Catholic Church in Ireland following the establishment of the Papal University of Maynooth?

As surmised above by Declan Kiberd, while the Gaelic order, plus its language and associated culture, retreated to the horizons of national consciousness, the one pillar of national identity that remained standing was the Roman Catholic religion. From the late medieval implantation of that identification to the portals of the 21st century, to be really Irish meant, for the majority of Irish people, being a loyal son or daughter of the Irish Roman Catholic Church and a faithful bearer of the latter's intellectual and devotional baggage.

English Roman Catholics such as Cardinal Newman, G.K. Chesterton and Hilaire Belloc were to provide the requisite academic and literary pabulum with which to nourish the minds of the Irish faithful in the first half of the 20th Century. The Church—aided and abetted by the State—saw to it that the works of "dissident" Irish scribes of the caliber of Oscar Wilde, Liam O'Flaherty, Seán Ó Faoláin, James Joyce, Bernard Shaw, Seán O'Casey and Frank O'Connor, et al., were censored and banned from sale accordingly in the Irish Free State.

Did the muted submissiveness of the Irish in the face of such intellectual bullying express the psychological conditioning of a people whose slavish attitudes, typical of colonized subjects, were largely unaffected by the physical departure of the old colonial master?

Could it be that a similar deference was transferred to a new, albeit spiritual, leader? And, if so, what was the mechanism employed to ensure that such a new loyalty could exceed that owed to the new temporal power?

THE POWER OF MAGICAL THINKING

The efficacy of the Church in leaving its stamp on Irish society can hardly be considered as remarkable, given that the State's education system was largely in clerical hands.

Thus, the catechism and Christian apologetics

became mandatory subjects in all schools under Church control. The upshot of this was that almost the entire population of the Irish Free State became subject to intensive Roman Catholic indoctrination, with its heavy emphasis on the virtues of complete and total submission to both the "temporal" and ecclesiastical orders, equated with resignation to the will of God.

Thence, disparagement of independent rational intellectual enquiry, even of matters outside the theological domain, accompanying unquestioning deference to its dogma and authority, became an obligatory sign of loyalty to that pillar of true Irish identity, the Roman Catholic Church.

The inevitable consequence of such an emphasis was the enhancement of acritical thought and normalization of the brooding submissiveness that characterizes colonized subjects everywhere. Thus, much of the psychological legacy of the First Colonization of the Irish Mind was conserved by ecclesiastical hegemonization of mainline intellectual discourse in Ireland for almost two centuries.

Thanks to the conflation of a militantly conservative Catholicism to essential Irishness, the primacy of dogmatic faith above reason, of magical rather than rational thinking, almost came to be mandatory national characteristics. Unfortunately, magical thinking—in whose remit natural phenomena become the plaything of occult forces—is not exclusive to matters of the soul, *sensu strictu*.

The cultural censorship instituted by the Free

State civil authorities in 1929 at the behest of the Catholic Hierarchy provided a suitably enclosed hothouse environment within which almost all non-Catholic ideology was excoriated, being, literally, of the devil.

When a national majority becomes infected with the virus of an irrational dogmatism, clear thought in whatever area of intellectual endeavor becomes unpatriotic or, at the least, highly suspect.

One consequence of this pervasive ecclesiastical hegemony was the condemnation of "alien" ideologies—socialism was one of such, according to one-time Taoiseach, Charlie Haughey—and a correspondingly lopsided political culture. Out of kilter with the European norm, it features *Tweedledum* and *Tweedledee*—two big right-wing parties, the now almost ideologically identical Fianna Fáil and Fine Gael—in an eternal ding-dong battle for power.

The traditional Left-Right configuration of traditional European politics failed to materialize significantly in Ireland. Left politics and, God forbid, communism were two of the politically ultraconservative Catholic Church's most reviled bogeymen. However, as ecclesiastical influence declines, support for Fine Gael and Fianna Fáil, the conservative bloc, appears now to be, finally, on the wane.

This political partisanship of the Church, the dominant ideological force in Irish society, was so extreme that the Vatican—the Irish Hierarchy following suit—encouraged the Irish people to support enthusiastically the fascist dictatorships of

Franco in Spain and Salazar in Portugal. It even encouraged the sending of a force of anti-Republican volunteers to fight in Spain against the forces of a democratically elected republican government there. Thence, the strains of the *Te Deum* that was celebrated in the Vatican to commemorate the defeat of Spanish democracy by the forces of General Franco would have echoed in many Irish hearts.

The impact of ecclesiastically-inspired inhibition of rational lay discourse made of 26-County Ireland an effectively closed society, economically and culturally, whose restrictive values were shielded from irradiation by modern secular thought by a rigorous literary and film censorship.

Access to the thought and literature of non-conforming Irish intellectuals was denied to the Irish people by confessional state bureaucrats, clerical and lay, in the role of guardians of faith, morals and intellectual orthodoxy. The exclusion of foreign heretical and immoral (i.e. often intellectual) material conformed to guidelines set by the Vatican's *Index Librorum Prohibitorum* (Index of Prohibited Books), until the latter was terminated by Pope Paul VI in 1966. However, the pendulum was to swing radically in the opposite direction.

Irrational and/or chaotic thought, incorporating groundless optimism/pessimism, are not states of mind confined to any one area of Irish life. This is hardly surprising, given that such a mental cast is of a piece with the colonizer's myth of the irrational, chaotic, Irish man/woman, as internalized by Irish colonial subjects over centuries of British colonial rule in Ireland.

As an American friend of mine once remarked: "I think of Ireland as the only country I know where a good story always trumps a good argument".

So, the Second Colonization of the Irish Mind, by discouraging rational thought, had the added effect of buttressing the colonizer's myth of gormless Paddy the Irishman.

COUNTERCURRENTS

Social, cultural and political movements invariably generate their dialectical opposites. So, it would be surprising if the pro-British influence of the Irish Roman Catholic Church was not tempered to some extent from within its own ranks.

Thus, Father John Murphy, parish priest of Boolavogue, County Wexford, stood with his parishioners in the 1798 Uprising against English rule, and in defiance of the Irish Roman Catholic Church that took the English side.

Father Michael Flanagan, the socialist priest who stood for the Republic in the Irish Civil War, the successful counter revolution and tragic sequel of the Irish War of Independence, was another priest who did not hesitate to translate Christian charity into direct political action.

There were many others, and still are, valiant Irish priests and nuns who have not hesitated to take a stand on behalf of the downtrodden and oppressed, both in Ireland and in distant mission fields.

Also, in spite of official Church attitudes towards Irish, a weak counter-current in favor of the language surfaced at different times within the native-speaking clergy, throwing up a number of doughty defenders. Seán Mac Éil (1791—1881), an Archbishop of Tuam, in the West of Ireland, insisted often on preaching in Irish to his flock. He compiled an Irish-language catechism and prayer book.

An tAthair Peadar Ó Laoghaire (1839-1920) is regarded as being one of the founders of modern literature in Irish. He is most remembered for his Faustian tale, *Séadhna*, and his autobiographical *Mo Scéal Féin*.

An tAthair Pádraig Ó Duinnín (1860–1934), was compiler of the most complete and unsurpassed compendium of Irish Gaelic lexicography and lore, *Focloir Uí Dhuinnín* – Dineen's Irish-English Dictionary, whose riches and occasionally quirky formulations have inspired generations of writers, both in Irish and English.

The invaluable contributions of many other priests, bishops, even a cardinal, lay brothers and nuns to the corpus of Irish Gaelic literature could be mentioned here, but such divulgation strays too far from the main theme of this monograph.

THE BITTER FRUITS OF SUBMISSION

In a case that came to light in 2014, 796 so-called "illegitimate" children of unmarried mothers in the care of the Bon Secours order of nuns, and possibly some adults also, rejects of a grimly uncharitable puritanical Irish Catholic society, died from disease and malnutrition.

As discovered by local amateur historian, Catherine Corless, some of their uncoffined corpses were buried secretly in a sewage tank. It seems since that she may have just uncovered the tip of a singularly ghastly iceberg. Ms. Corless was shocked by the fact that Irish news media showed little or no interest in the story (*The Guardian*, 4/6/2014).

Coming on the heels of the sensational clerical pederasty disclosures of recent years, and the international publicity given to the Church-sponsored Magdalene Homes misery of "fallen" women, the Irish Catholic Church became, once again, the target of knee-jerk anticlericalism and much publicly expressed wrath.

The Tuam care center was one of ten such centers in Ireland for unmarried mothers and their offspring, managed—in at least some cases—by seemingly unprepared lay persons and various orders of nuns. 30,000 children were adopted from these centers between 1922 and 1952. A further 45,000 children were adopted, many by U.S. couples, from these centers from 1952 onwards.

Given the magnitude of this human tragedy, anger at the Church is understandable. But, significantly, little of the public's ire was directed at a State that irresponsibly entrusted the care of such citizens to mainly Roman Catholic religious authorities. This State was fully cognizant of all that was happening in the primitive facilities of these Irish gulags. Its officials glibly attributed the abnormally high death rate of their juvenile recluses to the weak constitutions of the latter, an inevitable consequence of their illegitimacy, according to them, as reported by Irish media in June 2014.

At the bottom of this grim pyramid, however, was the extraordinary submissiveness of parents to the inhuman dictates of a Church-State machine that demanded the commitment of their "wayward" daughters, 75,000 of such "untouchables" according to press reports, and their offspring to such unloving, not to say brutal, "care".

Why then did Irish parents allow themselves to be browbeaten into meekly surrendering their own flesh and blood to the mercies of a "corrective "system that entailed isolation in horrible conditions behind grey walls both from their own flesh and blood and the population at large? How did such craven submissiveness ever become an integral part of what the Irish are?

Did a long-established pattern of behavior, internalized during years of forelock-tugging submission to the British Raj, translate itself seamlessly under the native dispensation into meek unquestioning obedience to the dictates of the almost unique moral code preached by the princely prelates of Holy Mother Church's Irish subsidiary and their secular accomplices?

No other explanation for the aberrant offspring-denying behavior of the parents of unmarried pregnant daughters appears to hold much water.

The enduring primacy of emotion and magical thinking, all too often privileged in Ireland over rational thinking, is part of the legacy of the Second Colonization of Ireland that endures.

But also, paradoxically, is the so-called Irish Sexual Revolution, a comparatively recent arrival on the national scene which along with the renowned Irish "drinking culture" so often astonishes—or appalls—visitors to present-day Ireland.

Both expressions of the new Ireland are to be observed in full flower in Temple Bar, Dublin's supposed cultural quarter, but are by no means confined to that location. Observation of Friday and Saturday night shenanigans there and elsewhere in Ireland confirm the ubiquity of this relatively recent phenomenon.

Such hedonistic indulgence is often seen as a liberating rebound from the puritanism of Irish Catholicism, and especially from the extreme sexual repression that marked the years of the ecclesiastical dominance of Irish society. This mandatory joylessness, as well as destroying the lives of thousands, introduced an element of social fragmentation into rural life. Its dark shadow had, arguably, the effect of enhancing the abundant economic motives that already existed for the flight to the cities and abroad from an often socially grim Irish countryside.

So, hardly surprisingly in view of all of such negativity, the Catholic Church is frequently scapegoated these days by anticlerical intellectuals for many of the ills that beset Irish society, especially in relation to emotional and sexual matters. Such criticism errs, almost invariably, in its over-simplicity. However, in the context of the compelling evidence just related, the fact that the Church has become the cynosure of much critical gazing is fully understandable.

Indeed, visceral hatred for the Irish Catholic Church deforms much social discourse and can go so far as to divert attention often from the more fundamental causes of the many social evils that beset the Irish body politic.

Thence, as in many such discussions, the gaze is averted all too often from the essential root of the evil—that 500 kilo gorilla sitting in the middle of the room, so to speak: SCIS, that enduring behavioral complex which came to configure the Irish psyche during centuries of intense English colonial rule.

As previously described, a marked sense of cultural inferiority, incorporating low self-esteem, unquestioning obedience and an immature submissiveness to all authority, clerical and lay, is an integral symptom of the Super-Colonized Irish Syndrome (SCIS).

The main "mortal sin" of the Catholic Church in this bleak context was to have aided and abetted the largely successful efforts of the colonizing power to delete the historic Irish identity, and the language that conformed that identity, from the memory banks of the colonized faithful.

Thus, it helped to replace that identity by a low-status outgroup Post-Gaelic identity whose psychological hallmark is SCIS. Its crusade to replace Gaelic

Catholicism with devotional exercises expressed in an alien tongue was of a piece with its anglicizing mission.

Simultaneously, an Irish Catholic Church, contaminated by the Jansenist heresy, promoted a perverse sexual and general morality that incongruously, in a wider Roman Catholic context, incorporated some of the most repressive behavioral and cultural norms that Protestant Victorian England was capable of generating.

Paradoxically, certain mid-20th century Irish language movement elements conflated their campaign on behalf of Irish to extreme ultra-Catholic beliefs and the narrow agenda of the Second Colonization of the Irish Mind.

This self-contradictory stance led to the identification of Irish speakers and the Irish language movement, in general, as being a cultural wing of what was perceived by progressive elements of Irish society to be an obscurantist counter-revolutionary religious force. This identification, for those who made it, accentuated the "hate" aspect of the neo-colonized Irish love/hate relationship with the Irish language.

This was especially true of the super-colonized stratum who either abhor or patronize all things Gaelic. It was also true of some of a Left political orientation—and most particularly if that orientation was internationalist in tone—who saw the Irish language as being an instrument of class oppression, expedited by the Catholic nationalist bourgeoisie, the seed bed of clerical vocations.

Be that as it may, the emerging Dionysian *ceol agus craic* (music and fun) image of contemporary popular Irish culture can be seen as a reaction against the inhibitory physical and intellectual constraints to which the Irish people were expected to conform in defense of a religious ethos whose basic tenets they are now increasingly inclined to disbelieve and, thence, to disobey.

This latter was increasingly perceived as being an expression of the anachronistic, medieval ideology of a confessional Irish state. Driven in the 1960s by the failure of its protectionist capitalist economy, the latter mutated into a new order defined by its open economy and media-mediated total permeability to all aspects of Anglosphere culture.

Rapidly developing media technology would make short work of what was left of the censorship barrier to the acquisition of knowledge of what the rest of the world thought, believed and did. Thus, secular thought and values began to percolate through Irish society and erode the ideological foundations of the pre-existing clerically dominated order.

The scene was now set for The Third Colonization of the Irish Mind.

THE THIRD COLONIZATION OF
THE IRISH MIND

MADE IN THE USA?

The Third Colonization of the Irish Mind by Anglosphere culture and values is still very much "in full swing" (said appropriately). Contemporary Irish cultural mores now largely conform—with some remaining light regional touches—to those of mainstream British Isles popular culture. Whatever regional specificity it retains largely pertains to GAA-promoted sports and some North American cultural influences mainly specific to Ireland and Irish America.

Thus, the distinctively American flavor of Ireland's contemporary St. Patrick's Day celebrations and the still faintly lingering Hollywood (*Darby O'Gill and the Little People, The Quiet Man, Going My Way, etc.*) and Kennedy factors.

This link is reinforced by periodic visits from such honorary "Irishmen" as Bill Clinton, Tom Cruise and Barak Obama, together with members of the Kennedy family and various Hollywood and show-biz luminaries signaling that the U.S.A., with all its works and pomps has become an integral part of what we Irish now are. The U.S. Independence Day (July 4th) and Thanksgiving (the fourth Thursday of November) have established Irish niches for themselves and, thus, seem to be well on its way to becoming Irish celebratory events.

Maybe it was always destined to be so! In the

popular Irish imaginary, North America is the land that welcomed the starving Irish, and in whose mythical melting pot they worked, thrived and earned their place in the sun.

However genial this picture appears to be, it does not concur with a much less pleasant and entertaining reality. For, the ragged immigrant Irish, fresh off the coffin ships of Famine times, were despised, mercilessly exploited and treated with cynical brutality by their American "hosts" and, very often, even by their own kind! Irish immigrants were selected for death-dealing labor in canal and railway construction in the U.S. South rather than Negro slaves, being adjudged to be more expendable than the latter.

However, such unpleasantness has no place in the idyllic narrative of Pat and Mary making hay while the sun shines on *"the shores of Amerikay.*"*

So, the harsh realities of the suffering immigrant Irish in America were eclipsed by the wish-fulfilling myth of the hearty and friendly acceptance of our emigrant "huddled masses" by the American natives. The USA, as viewed from Ireland, seemed—and still seems—the land of freedom, equal opportunity, where merit, application and hard work always finds their just reward.

Thence, the prevalence of pictures of the pathologically

---

*Those who are captivated by romanticized images of Irish emigrants in the U.S. would do well to arm themselves with *How the Irish became White,* by Noel Ignatiev, to correct their misperception of what was, in fact, a grim historical saga.

profligate John F. Kennedy, accompanied sometimes by his spouse, the promiscuous Jackie, paired quite incongruously with whatever Pope, usually Pius XII or John XXIII, that still adorn the walls of some rural Irish living rooms. Not to mention the fact that a picture of the same "Saint" JFK graces a wall of Galway's Cathedral![*]

Thus, the U.S.A. seems to many Irish people— especially to those with relatives living there— almost like a western extension of Ireland. Or, conversely, contemporary Ireland could be an eastern extension of the U.S.A. Thence the ready availability and acceptance in Ireland of U.S. pop-culture products— cinema, TV programs, popular music, all emanating from North America.

Eavesdropping on conversations on Dublin's commuter train service, the DART, yields the intelligence that BBC and other British television channel products are more popular in Ireland—and talked about—than those of their Irish counterparts. Irish television carries an extensive load of soaps, situation comedies and films of varied sources: almost exclusively of Anglosphere origin—Britain, the U.S.A., Australia and New Zealand—whose main common denominator is the shared set of assumptions and stereotypes that define the

---

[*]Readers who doubt the applicability of these adjectives to the flawed U.S.A. Camelot saga lead actors should consult *One Nation Under Sex: How the Private Lives of Presidents, First Ladies and Their Lovers Changed the Course of American History,* Larry Flynt and David Eisenbach, Palgrave Macmillan Trade, 2011.

Anglosphere way of life. And which have now come to be an integral part of what we Irish are these days! So, how did all of this massive Cultural Revolution come about?

POST-PROTECTIONISM'S CULTURAL FALLOUT

This Third Colonization of The Irish Mind, pertains basically to the invasion of, or absorption by, the Irish psyche of contemporary Anglosphere consumerist values that arrive as both overt and subliminal components of the cultural products referred to above.

This process began in earnest during the sixties of the last century following the opening of the unsustainable stagnant protected capitalist Irish economy to international capital. This initiative was largely the result of the efforts of one civil servant— the economist, T.K. Whittaker and one politician, the then Taoiseach, Seán Lemass.

In tandem with the development of national television, such an innovative aperture to the outside world of a hitherto closed, culturally moribund and almost hermetically sealed society had profound implications for all aspects of Irish life. The subliminal components of the sustained Anglosphere media barrage inevitably eroded the foundations of the secular and ecclesiastical ideologies that had cemented together the confessional Irish state. What was destined to take their place?

An ideological vacuum! For, the consequences of

the First Colonization of The Irish Mind, and their subsequent amplification by the Second Colonization, had left Ireland bereft of a credible secular counter-ideology with which it might have developed a (now notional) cultural, social and economic specificity to counteract the worst excesses of the emerging socio-economic order.

Teilifís Éireann (Irish national television) commenced its transmissions on New Year's Eve 1961 and always has been, along with the wide range of TV viewing options now available, a key modernizing influence. The individualistic values with which it irradiated its viewers were enthusiastically adopted by the dominant sections of Irish society. This cultural mutation was facilitated by Celtic Tiger affluence, while it lasted, and by the loss of the previously dominant moral authority of the Irish Roman Catholic Church.

The latter might have provided a countervailing moral force to the rampant "greed is good" individualism ushered in by the "Tiger" had it not lost popular credibility, coming to grief on the criminal concupiscence of elements of its clergy, on the flouting of the nation's civil law by some clerics and on what was perceived to be the rocks of its own hypocrisy, corruption and arrogance.

Electronic communications technology and Anglosphere entertainment programs rapidly eroded the ideological residuum of the two previous colonizations and, concomitantly, what little now remains of the Irish language and its culture.

The effect of English-language television on

transgenerational transmission of Irish in the *Gaeltacht* was devastating. Families, whose contact with spoken English had been mainly limited to association with summer visitors and Irish College students, now had a permanent English speaker—the television set—installed as a de facto part of the family.

Thus, the abnormal, the English language, now became part of the new bilingual normal in living rooms and pubs. The boundary between the two languages was breached and *Géarla* was born. Code-switching, a jumping back and forth between Irish and English, gradually established itself as the conversational norm, both in the *Gaeltacht* and, among Irish speakers in the rest of the country.

The part-Irish-language TV station located in the Conamara *Gaeltacht*, now TG4, arrived too late—and with too meager a program repertoire—to seriously dent viewer loyalty to the earlier established English-language stations.

With the later ready availability of British television in Ireland—and especially sports channels—the objects of TV loyalty became more diversified. The installation of satellite dish systems beaming in programs from all over the world was to even further multiply the range of choice.

In the meantime, an increasing share of the viewing time of what was originally hoped to be an all-Irish-language television station was now devoted to programming in English.

Thus, large sections of the population in general,

not only the young, unburdened all too often by even the most superficial knowledge of Ireland's political, social and cultural history and ideals, become effortlessly assimilated to Anglosphere cultural and behavioral norms.

THE BROKEN THREAD

Irish history, now only an elective subject of both the Junior and Senior Cycles, is taught only in nonlinearly sequenced chronological episodes. The latter approach was defended to me by a history teacher on the basis that Jean-Francois Lyotard, and other now discredited apostles of postmodernism, a philosophical wing of neo-liberalism, had "disproved" the validity of all metanarratives.

In the meantime, the cultural/linguistic dynamic, that developed over centuries, of the relation between colonizer and colonized in British Ireland—indispensable for understanding the rationale for decolonization and language re-possession, is completely ignored in school texts. The disappearance of the language is even described with cynical glibness (or, maybe, just plain ignorance) in school history notes I have seen as being, simply, one side-effect of the Great Famine.

This lacuna, which applies even to *Gaelscoileanna* and *Gaeltacht* schools, has always had critically serious implications for the transgenerational transmission of Irish. For, by depriving students of a cultural/linguistic counter-narrative to the official story (or nonstory), to which young—and not only young—Irish speakers could relate personally, it automatically aborts the potential ideological basis of that vigorous non-aggressive cultural élan vitally needed to construct and/or sustain any viable linguistic/ cultural discourse alternative to that being promoted ceaselessly by the dominant Anglosphere media.

In this ideologically "sanitized" context, the words of Renato Constantino, describing the legacy of colonialism in the Philippines, as he addresses himself to the implications of such contemporary ahistoricity, has relevance for Irish educators concerned with transmitting the Irish-language alternative to a younger generation:

"We see our present with as little understanding as we view our past because aspects of the past which could illumine the present have been concealed from us. This concealment has been effected by a systematic process of mis-education characterized by a thoroughgoing inculcation of colonial values and attitudes—a process which could not have been so effective had we not been denied access to the truth and to part of our written history. As a consequence, we have become a people without a sense of history. We accept the present as given, bereft of historicity. Because we have so little comprehension of our past, we have no appreciation of its meaningful inter-relation with the present."

The Nigerian novelist and Nobel prizewinner, Wole Soyinka eloquently describes the critical role of the repossession of historical knowledge in the task of national recovery:

"It involves, very simply, the conscious activity of recovering what has been hidden, lost, repressed, denigrated, or indeed simply denied by ourselves—yes by ourselves also—but definitely by the conquerors of our peoples and their Eurocentric bias of thought and relationships... For a people to develop they must have constant recourse to their own history. Not an uncritical recourse but definitely a recourse. To deny them the existence of this therefore has a purpose, for it makes them neutered objects on whose tabula rasa, that clean slate of the mind, the text of the master race—cultural, economic, religious and so on—can be inscribed. A logical resistance counterstrategy therefore develops; true nationalists find themselves, at one stage or another and at varying levels, confronted with a need to address the recovery of their history and culture... breeding a newly aware humanity equipped with the strategies of the experience-laden journey from its beginnings to its present."

But what relevance have these prescriptions today for young Irish people, whose lives revolve increasingly around video games, laptop, tablet and TV screens—which in very many cases, has replaced school and parental tutelage as their major formative influence—and for whom such attenuated Irishness as exists is already sinking into that common consumerist Anglosphere melting pot, sometimes referred to as "global youth culture?"

SCHOOL IS A TV SCREEN

Following marketing determined trends set by their counterparts, and role models, in Great Britain and the U.S.A., the strongest cultural referents of Irish teen media tend increasingly to be the latest U.S. celebrities, English or Scottish football teams, the pop culture personalities that people British and American entertainment shows and soaps, video games, the content of youth culture magazines, etc.

In a similar vein, for most young Irish people today, Irishness—when such is considered relevant—is most likely to be symbolized by sundry show business personalities along with sports teams, all of whom have widespread media exposure. Although the main claim of these worthies to fame is, usually, to have achieved acceptance, and made megabucks (or pounds sterling), in Britain and the wider Anglosphere world, their usually vacuous comments on current affairs sometimes get more exposure than those of the Taoiseach.

Regarding Irishness, Michael Collins is a passing exception to the above trend—thanks to Neil Jordan (and Liam Neeson) he had the good fortune to be "immortalized" by becoming a celluloid hero.

Ireland is not unique in this respect. Given the global reach of neo-liberalism and its associated media culture, similar economic and cultural change is coming to encompass almost the entire globe. However, the susceptibility of an almost monoglot Anglophone Ireland to rampant consumerism and monoculture is greater than is the case with most other nations, given the absence in Ireland of the cultural filter of any significant countervailing culture or language that might configure incoming information to fit specifically Irish norms.

In this context, it is relevant to mention that Irish people now spend 3h and 32minutes, as a daily average, sitting in front of TV sets. According to the same article[*] 629,000 households have TV screen sizes of 40 inches or more and:

"Television drives conversations–if you are not watching a popular programme, you're missing out on the conversation."

Missing out on what?

COLONIZATION'S WINNERS AND LOSERS

The strength of neoliberal consumer culture is seen in its ability to quickly and successfully impose its hegemony of its values on societies even well beyond the physical borders of Anglophonia.

Due to the global reach of electronic media and advances in dubbing technology, linguistic borders no longer serve to completely insulate populations against the all-pervasive influence of current Anglosphere culture.

This impressive power is seen graphically in its contribution to the double cultural colonization of much of the population of the former East German state, the German Democratic Republic (GDR), after its annexation

---

[*]*Irish Independent* online 5/7/2014.

in 1990 by West Germany. The cultural metamorphosis that accompanied that economic and political take-over was described to me by a former citizen of the GDR as follows:

"You see some of this cultural and largely willing sellout and self-destruction (by former GDR citizens) in a specifically an East German rush to be as quickly and rapidly assimilated into West Germany as possible.

And then there is the wider fact of a growing Americanization of all of Germany e.g. young children don't know the German Grimm fairy tales anymore, or very rudimentary - they know all about Disney characters, Winnie the Pooh and the characters they are fed from Anglo-US TV.

Amazingly, even the German Weihnachtsmann who used to always arrive in person on Xmas eve from the winter forest now inexplicably arrives flying through the night sky and apparently squeezes through non-existent chimneys into non-existing fireplaces..."

Parenthetically, it might be asked: how many Irish children, even Irish-speaking ones, know a tenth as much (to be hopelessly optimistic) about the Fianna and Red Branch heroes of traditional Gaelic mythology, Fionn Mac Cumhail and Cúchulain, as they do about *The Simpsons, Dora the Explorer, Sponge Bob Squarepants,* etc., and the world of Disney? How many even recall the English refrain of Irish children in Halloween doorways: *"Any apples or nuts?...Any apples or nuts?"* now almost universally replaced by its U.S.A. equivalent, *"Trick or*

Treat!" or remember the home-produced Halloween disguises of yesteryear supplanted by the current plastic "made in China" Dracula and Superman outfits?

"The East to West German cultural dissolution has a linguistic dimension; there are particular shibboleths whereby an East German would be identifiable. All East Germans eager not to be identified as 'losers' avoid using these forms: e.g. if you say 'Plaste' *instead of* 'Plastik', *you are East German, if you say* 'Kaufhalle' *instead of* 'Supermarkt', *you are East German, if you don't pronounce the word* 'Restaurant' *with a French accent but a German one, you are East German.*

In terms of historical understanding: if you refer to the societies of ancient Greece and Rome as 'Sklavenhalterordnung' *(slave holding societies) rather than* 'Antike' *(antiquity) and the Middle Ages as* 'Feudalordnung' *(feudal order) rather than* 'Mittelalter', *you are East German, having gone to school in the German Democratic Republic.*

If you remember the Danish comedy series 'Olsenbande' *but not the American series* 'Lassie', *then you are East German. In fact, if you have heard of Soviet writers, you are East German, and if you learnt at school that capitalism experiences cyclical crises and are in no way surprised when this happens, you grew up in the German Democratic Republic."*

Considering how one's world-view is shaped by words, ponder the fact that in Ireland a complete language has almost entirely disappeared to be replaced by that of a colonizing power and its accompanying baggage!

"In the new Germany, certain words disappeared altogether from official usage, for example: Frieden (peace), Völkerfreundschaft (friendship among peoples) and Solidarität (solidarity). In fact, references to these in the public arena invariably date back to GDR times.

After unification, many of the streets bearing the names of anti-fascists were changed. So, for example, Hans-Beimler-Strasse *turned into* Otto-Braun-Strasse. *(Beimler, was a Communist Party deputy who died in the Spanish Civil War; Otto Braun, a Social Democratic politician was Prime Minister of Prussia between 1920 to 1932). The city of* Karl-Marx-Stadt *reverted to its former name* Chemnitz. *East Germany called the Nazis* 'fascists,' *while in the FGR, they continued to be referred to be referred to as* 'national socialists' *(and* 'fascism' *euphemistically as* 'national socialism'*). Thus, socialism was equated with fascism, squaring with the main purpose of the re-writing of history in the new Germany."*

This account of place-name replacement in the former GDR squares with colonialism's strategy of inducing collective amnesia in subject populations by changing histories, old customs, languages, even place-names.

The latter ploy, in an Irish context, was described by Brian Friel in his play, *Translations*, in which an Irish landscape is comprehensively "Englished" by operatives of the colonizing power.

A conspicuous symptom of the Irish colonized mentality is seen clearly in place-name signposting. Outside the official *Gaeltacht*, the original Irish name is almost universally displayed with a smaller font size, in italics, often bowdlerized and illegible to those with less than average eyesight. But, to conclude my East German informant's remarks:

"Those who wish not to be identified as East German don't give themselves away by saying such words. It should be mentioned that there is also awareness and resistance to this, but it is unlikely it'll outlast the generations with a living memory.

Already, the generation that were teenagers when the GDR collapsed and was annexed, have learnt the new history so well that they receive prizes from the ruling class for the perfect way in which they present their past lives - as victims of a dictatorship."

Does the apparent present relationship between the Irish and their past reflect a similar collective amnesia? And what does such this putative urge to forget the past tell us about the origins of the current collective Irish self-image?

DANCE, PUPPET, DANCE!

"What we have seen in the United States and a number of other countries since the 1970s is the emergence of a savage form of free market fundamentalism, often called neo-liberalism, in which there is not only a

deep distrust of public values, public goods and public institutions but the embrace of a market ideology that accelerates the power of the financial elite and big business while gutting those formative cultures and institutions necessary for a democracy to survive. The commanding institutions of society in many countries, including the United States, are now in the hands of powerful corporate interests, the financial elite and right-wing bigots whose strangulating control over politics renders democracy corrupt and dysfunctional. More specifically, Americans now live in what the new Pope has condemned as the 'tyranny of unfettered capitalism,' where the corporate, financial, and ruling elites shape politics, assault unions, mobilize great extremes of wealth and power, and enforce a brutalizing regime of neo-liberalism. This is a period that lacks any sense of social and economic justice, a historical moment in which the existing norms, values, and for that matter language itself legitimate the production of zones of social and civil death, death spheres—driven by a mad violence rooted in a dystopian theater of cruelty."

Henry Giroux

In the so-called developed world up to the 1960s, consumerism—a way of life based on the consumption of the ephemeral—was mainly confined to the bourgeoisie. However, from then on, it gradually extended itself to all social strata, implanting a taste for novelty, excess and frivolity, "retail therapy", along with the cults of personal development and physical wellbeing.

In short: the ideology of individualistic hedonism became rooted in the masses of the so-called developed world, including Ireland.

Technological novelty and the corresponding necessary seduction of consumers by things came to seem to be more credible motors of social movement than the classical notions of alienation and class struggle.

So as consumerism becomes institutionalized throughout the entire capitalist ambit, the creation of artificial needs and its rational manipulation of society, in all its aspects, including the individual's private life, become essential to the maximization of profit, the *raison d'etre* of the whole capitalist edifice.

How this globalized consumerist life style affects the mentality of its adherents has been studied in depth, notably in Europe by sociologists such as Gilles Lipovetsky (France), Zygmunt Baumann (Poland and Britain), Henry Giroux (U.S.A.), et al.

They point out that through the mediacy of commodities, promoted by highly aggressive targeted marketing, and offering the possibility of an infinite number of new sensations, consumers establish a new relation with their own existence, which profoundly affects their personal, political and cultural behavior.

The fear of the boredom of repetition, of one's life becoming stale, impels the consumer cult member to buy in order to self-renovate. Get out there and buy if you want to be "with it".

The consumerist subject is described as being cool, adaptable, a lover of pleasure and individual liberties in the here and now, an enemy of the tedium of effort and deferred rewards.

He is often a self-obsessed narcissist who fears ageing and self-medicates correspondingly. In the new consumerist order, hedonism is legitimated and exalted. One is invited to "loosen up" and "get a life".

"Greed is good!" is the contemporary mantra. Individual salvation is in the search for novelty and associated stimulations and sensations generated by the promised rich and full life so created.

The legitimacy of past strictures have been neutralized by the unquestioned and unquestionable imperative of private individual satisfaction.

As this hedonistic individualism *a la carte* becomes rampant in consumerist societies, such as that of modern Ireland, established political and cultural discourses lose their legislative authority. Veneration and respect for tradition is replaced by a passion for the "new" and the "present", now identified with the "good". The "old" is excoriated while the "young/new" is deified.

Society becomes relatively indifferent to the public good and any serious sense of social responsibility. The egoism of "every man for himself" takes precedence over the latter.

Contemporary urban man, as one social commentator, Richard Sennett, has pointed out, has become refractory to participating in collective action not devoted to the promotion of his private pleasure. Thence social conflicts that emerge in these times, with few exceptions, seldom address themselves to objectives of general interest, but rather towards the defense of particular interests. Thus, we witness the preponderance of sectorial egoisms over joint searches for overall social justice.

Capitalism's manipulation of communications media plays a key role in reproducing a society based on the presently dominant values of individualistic hedonism and autonomy. By continually transmitting information, often disguised advertising, concerning social life, politics, sexuality, diet, sports, economics, psychology, spirituality, medicine, technological innovation, theatre, rock groups,etc., they are more powerful promoters of formation and social integration than State and formal schooling.

By playfully promoting the culture of universal relativity and the celebration of hedonism, mass media have dissolved the force of tradition, old notions of class, social solidarity and moralities imposed by religious and political ideologies that were referential for previous generations.

Traditional Irish language revivalist ideology, hence the Irish language itself, seems to hard-core consumerists to have lost all contact with the new universe of thought and feeling in which they feel comfortably at home. The world of radical politics and serious social protest seems, to all but a thoughtful and discerning minority, a strange and foreign place, the haunt of antisocial weirdoes.

For, submission to behavioral norms mandated by the narratives and ideals of the past is incompatible with the contemporary concept of the individual as being a fully-independent freely-choosing master of his own destiny.

Such personal freedom may well have its own virtues. However, the individualistic social indifference it generates may amplify some negative behavioral tendencies associated with our colonial heritage, notably that passive cynicism that so frequently corrodes any possibility of effective social, cultural and political action.

The value-free hipster mentality also provides a climate within which compulsive behaviors-substance abuse, criminality, sexual crime and gratuitous violence can flourish. Day-to-day media reports make us vividly aware that such negativity must be increasingly integrated into a complete profile of contemporary Irishness.

Henry Giroux summarizes the effects of neo-liberal indoctrination on the North America population:

"Not only has democracy been undermined and transformed into a form of authoritarianism unique to the twenty-first century, but there is also an existential crisis that is evident in the despair, depoliticization, and crisis of subjectivity that has overtaken much of the population, particularly since 9/11 and the economic crisis of 2007. The economic crisis is not matched by a crisis of ideas and many people have surrendered to a neo-liberal ideology that limits their sense of agency by defining them primarily as consumers, subjects them to a pervasive culture of fear, blames them for problems that are not of their doing, and leads them to believe that violence is the only mediating force available to them, thus the pleasure quotient is

colonized and leads people to assume that...violence is the only way in which they can feel any type of emotion and pleasure. How else to interpret polls that show that a majority of Americans support the death penalty, government surveillance, drone warfare, the prison-industrial complex, and zero tolerance policies that punish children. Trust, honor, intimacy, compassion, and caring for others are now viewed as liabilities, just as self-interest has become more important than the general interest and common good. Selfishness, self-interest, and an unchecked celebration of individualism have become, as Joseph E. Stiglitz has argued, 'the ultimate form of selflessness.' What we are witnessing is an existential crisis rooted in the destruction of meaningful solidarities, supportive collective provisions, and the eradication of all public spheres that open up spaces for critical and compassionate public connections. One consequence of neo-liberalism is that it makes a virtue of producing a collective existential crisis, a crisis of agency and subjectivity, one that saps democracy of its vitality. The economic crisis intensified its worse dimensions, but the source of the crisis lies in the roots of neo-liberalism, particularly since its inception since the 1970s when social democracy proved unable to curb the crisis of capitalism and economics became the driving force of politics."

In short, the world of contemporary capitalism, Ireland included (the U.S.A. being Irish neo-liberalism's guiding economic beacon), has reached a point in which the commercialization of almost every aspect of human existence (predicted brilliantly by Karl Marx and

Friedrich Engels in their *Communist Manifesto*) no longer encounters structural, cultural or ideological obstacles. It is a society in which the whole gamut of social and personal life is being reorganized to conform to the logic of consumption, with all of the consequences, both positive and negative.

Money, the earning and spending of it, has moved to the dead center of the stage of human concern. As is inevitable in such a scenario, the public welfare and republican democracy itself are not only forced to take a back seat but open advocacy of them is well on the road to becoming criminalized in leading Anglosphere domains.

Large-scale corruption, together with its concomitant unjust and egregiously unequal distribution of socially-created wealth, follows the installation of what is, effectively, the rule of an oligarchic cabal, shamelessly flaunting the colors of liberal (effectively neo-conservative) democracy, effectively a "greed is good" regime.

Well-publicized events in Ireland in recent times demonstrate just how accurate a description of contemporary Irish society that is.

SURE, WHAT CAN WE DO?

How and when the consumerist mentality, superimposing itself on a pre-existing neocolonial mindset, will affect the Irish response to the neoliberal onslaught has still to be gauged.

The heretofore passive apathetic public answer, to Troika-imposed austerity measures, compared with that of other peripheral European countries, has been commented upon by the international press. There have been organized demonstrations, but nothing like on the scale, or with the frequency, of protests in the southern European periphery.

The clearly evident signs of social dereliction—massive emigration, the escalating problem of homelessness and sleeping rough, the progressive impoverishment of working people wherever Troika dictates are implemented, in Ireland and elsewhere, has led to massive protests and new political developments in other peripheral EU countries (such as Greece, Spain and Portugal). Why not in Ireland?

COULD IT REALLY BE BIOLOGICAL?

Could this passive submission to Troika dictates be directly related to SCIS, this hypothetical bye-product of Ireland's long tragic history? A more detailed examination of a putative biological dimension of the colonized mindset should leave us in a better position to assess what seems to be, on the face of it, a most unlikely hypothesis.

It is now known that trauma of the type suffered by the Irish people in the course of its colonization by England, can induce permanent psychological change in traumatized colonial populations. Both Franz Fanon and Albert Memmi, referred to earlier, were early investigators of this phenomenon. However much information has been garnered in this and related fields, especially neurobiology and genetics, since they published the results of their ground-breaking pioneering studies.

Thus, consideration of what is now known about the psychology of the colonization process is mandatory if we wish to canvass approaches that will enable us to better understand that affective and behavioral complex that characterizes many Irish people and gives a distinctive, and not always positive, flavor to the life of our nation.

THE PSYCHOLOGY OF COLONIZATION

THE STOCKHOLM SYNDROME: A METAPHOR FOR IRISHNESS?

"I don't think anybody is listening to them (i.e. proposers of economic alternatives) in Ireland and I don't hear any discussion there... because there's a herd instinct there, as you say, with Stockholm Syndrome. You've adopted the view of your oppressors, as if somehow they'll be nice to you, if you'll only give more money to them. You may need another 60% of your population to emigrate before you realize there may be an alternative."

So said US economist, Michael Hudson, as he discussed Irish docility in the face of EU economic oppression (*The Ruination of Ireland*, Counterpunch ,17/2/ 2014).

Hudson's equation of Irish acquiescence to economic blackmail and the Stockholm Syndrome, a case-proven psychological condition, is probably just only a convenient metaphor with which to highlight the strange reluctance of Irish financial and political establishments to face down their "betters", in this case the Irish bank's European creditors.[*]

---

[*] Such obsequiousness came with a heavy cost. According to Eurostat, Ireland, with less than 1 per cent of Europe's population, paid 43 per cent of the net cost of the banking crisis across all 27 EU member states - €41bn out of €96.2bn. That means that the cost of the bank bailout was €8,956 for every man, woman and child in Ireland, compared to an EU average of €191.

In this context, the most surprising aspect of this scenario noted by observers was the resigned and submissive response to this egregious injustice of a people that sees itself, apparently, fated to be a perpetual loser in any transaction with external powers. While Troika-imposed cuts in social spending brought angry millions on to the streets in Southern Europe, and generated new radical political formations, the Irish masses remained comparatively inert; the obligatory protest was muted as they settled into a disgruntled compliance with the "new abnormal".

Thus, if the Stockholm Syndrome (SS) is, indeed, a metaphor, it is a highly appropriate one with which to encapsulate the mindset of colonized subjects whose desire it is to please the master, whoever he may be, and hang the consequences. That such a people no longer desire to rescue their languages and cultures from oblivion, as they rush to embrace the language and customs of once-hated oppressors, can hardly surprise anyone.

But what exactly is this Stockholm Syndrome? Victims of the condition are traumatized hostages who come to empathize with their captors, to the point of identifying with them. The syndrome is named after a 1973 bank robbery in Stockholm, in which bank employees were held hostage for 6 days. This syndrome involves the growth of strong emotional ties between two persons where one person intermittently harasses, beats, threatens, abuses, or intimidates the other. These bank employee victims even defended their captors after being freed. The occurrence of this syndrome has been recorded for many other similar stressful contexts.

The Stockholm Syndrome is not, as far as is known, transmitted to the victim's offspring. Cultural transmission of symptoms of the condition can hardly be discounted, given the propensity of the young to imitate the behavior and affective attitudes of their elders, but such a transmission has not been demonstrated to date.

But what better metaphor to present-day Irish bonding with the English by those who never experienced English oppression—with all of its tortures, slaughter of prisoners, hangings, decapitations, rapes, eviscerations, castrations, evictions, coffin ships—at first hand?

Apart from rejection of their ancestral language by the present generation of Irish, their submissive emotionally-charged response to members of the British royals and other symbols of British power evidences a Stockholm-Syndrome-like condition. Visitors note the widespread Irish interest in English sport and popular culture, facilitated by the ready availability in Ireland of British print and electronic media. The huge number of Irish people, along with those of Irish descent, living in Britain and integrated into the British way of life, cannot but strengthen such bonding.

Then again, imitation of the "cultivated speech" of SE England, often regarded in Ireland as "educated", rapidly replacing what remains of Hiberno-English (often seen as a clownish rustic dialect), is convincingly explicable in terms of a Stockholm Syndrome-type bonding between descendants of the historic colonizer and his colonized Irish subjects. Indeed, some contemporary Dublin 4 (D4) speech seems to represent, with some ineradicable Irish touches, a subconsciously attempted assimilation to the SE English norm. In any case, it has become *de rigeur* for many present-day Irish professionals and media folk.

Approaching this relationship from another angle, the fact that the drunken, repugnant, ape-like "Paddy" of the 19th century Punch cartoons, resurrected in more recent times by English print, radio and television media, has become a popular fun figure, if not a social behavior model, for some Irish people, cannot but be of some social and political significance.

The etiology of this stereotype is described in detail in Josep T. Leersens' splendid *Mere Irish and Fíor Ghael* (Field Day, 1986) and will not be recapitulated here. What interests us is that the behavior of the colonized Irish subject has come to conform to the colonizer's stereotype of him. In other words, he literally mutates into his image as seen through the eyes of the English colonizer, no matter how self-demeaning that image is. Examples of such abound.

In fiction, the sycophantic Irish "house niggers" of Somerville and Ross's *The Irish RM* stories, serving "the quality" (the significantly named descendants of English colonizers) in the West of Ireland at the turn of the last century, charmed English and Irish readers of that epoch. These stories imaged the super-colonized Irish as gormless, sly but charming, needing the colonizers firm, but kindly, guiding hand. It morphed into a highly successful television series screened in Ireland and Britain in the 1980s.

A less benign image of the Irish as fools and stupid and/or drunken "Paddies", whose chaotic existences are redeemed by the fey leprechaunish charm they exhibit, was peddled by the British Channel 4 *Father Ted* television series. These episodes were popular with the lampooned Irish, who so enjoy these absurdly grotesque caricatures of themselves that the series was retransmitted by RTÉ 2, an Irish television channel.

The most interesting aspect of these entertainment tastes is that the obvious offensiveness of these portrayals seem to be invisible to a significant number, if not most, Irish people. Could we label this quirkiness as the "Sense of Humor of the Super-Colonized?" Of a low-status outgroup hell-bent on conserving its position within a neocolonial status quo?

Significantly, this "ability to laugh at (such offensive images of) ourselves" appears not to be shared by the black communities of the U.S.A. and Britain, for example, nor by Latino communities and indigenous Americans, et al. Jewish groups are always quick to denounce Shylock-like caricatures of their people. They rightly figure that such negative "entertainment" serves to establish and copper-fasten injurious prejudices against them on the part of the wider community.

Not so the modern Irish, however!

These Irish entertainment tastes co-exist with

acceptance of "sanitized" expressions of native culture (*Riverdance*, ballad singers, traditional music, etc.), where sanitization equals Anglosphere approval. But no *sean-nós* singing, for God's sake!

The almost invariable Irish media categorization of combatants in the most recent conflict in Northern Ireland bespeaks yet more evidence of a deep internalization of the colonizer's world view. Thus, while soldiers of the British Army were referred to as such, "soldiers" (even in cases where they were proven to have murdered civilians in cold blood), republican soldiers of the IRA were, and still are, invariably referred to as "terrorists", strictly conforming to the British press protocol.

In the same vein, a recent publicly funded video dealing, allegedly, with the origins of modern Ireland managed to avoid naming the leaders of the 1916 Rising, the foundational act of the Irish State, while featuring the ubiquitous Bono (listed in 2002 as one of the 100 greatest Britons), Sir Bob Geldof KBE, David Cameron and the English Queen, along with an appropriately unintelligible "Irish-language" version of the 1916 Proclamation.

The almost inevitable equation of "Irish" with inferior, absurd, gormless, and even dirty in present-day Irish speech, in both Irish (check *Gaelach* in Dinneen's Irish-English dictionary!) and in English, once again, and tellingly, bespeaks a generalized internalization of a culturally inferior national self-image, fully congruent with the Fanon-Memmi paradigm. Can contemporary Irishness be seen, in fact, as being anything other than neo-colonized (or super-colonized) Irishness, an invention of the English colonizer?

On the flip side of this cultural coin, Irish Gaelic is usually treated in much of "polite" Irish society as an outdated relic of another age, as embarrassingly uncouth, uncool, a useless 'bog-language'. Conversely, it may be patronizingly accepted as a fascinating residue of a charming folk culture, a quaint ancient tongue: *"It is lovely to hear it still being spoken"*. Alas and more is the pity, it doesn't fit the techno-savvy image which 21st century Ireland is hell-bent on projecting.

But if the Stockholm Syndrome does not appear to be inherited, how can the enduring strength of SCIS, as indicated by the many symptoms just described, be accounted for, almost a century after the English colonizer took his leave?

PADDY'S BROOD

The dominant Irish nationalist historical narrative holds that 26 Irish counties exited British colonialism when the Irish Free State was founded in 1922. How, then, did obvious psychological residues of colonization manage to survive and thrive under the conditions of a putative political independence?

One possibility is that learned submissive attitudes and behavioral patterns characteristic of colonized indigenous peoples are transmitted culturally (i.e. by the imitation by one generation of the attitudes and habits of its elders) from one generation to the next, culminating in today's Irishness. But, if that were the mode of transmission, one might have expected a certain attenuation of the symptoms of SCIS as successive generations further distanced themselves in time from the original causal agent, the suffering caused by the English colonial order. That didn't happen.

There may be another reason, then, for the strength with which SCIS manifests itself in contemporary Ireland.

Conforming with what has recently come to light, and what we now know, about the transgenerational transmission of genetic/epigenetic material that determines behavioral traits that we associate with SCIS, the overwhelming strength of the survival of colonized behavior in Ireland may very well point to its having a possible genetics/epgenetic basis, at least to some significant extent.

The genetics of Irishness seems may be one crucial area to investigate, if we are to fully account for one possible etiology of SCIS. In plainer language, could salient features of the latter condition be determined—at least, partially— by the very hereditary material of the Irish? Could contemporary Irishness be encoded for Irish DNA or associated epigenes.

As discussion of the latter question involves use of a terminology that may be unfamiliar to most readers, there follows below a brief summary of those aspects of cell biology that explain how the characteristics of persons, and living organisms in general, are determined and transmitted to their descendants.

Some may find this material to be somewhat dense. But as it is germane to the hypothesis being suggested in this essay, readers are urged not to surrender to the temptation to skip it.

Inheritance of the fear of the smell of acetophenone, the scent of which is reminiscent of cherries and almonds, was studied in laboratory mice. Male mice were exposed to the scent, while being given electric shocks. The animals learned to associate the scent with pain, shuddering in the presence of acetophenone even without a shock. This reaction was passed on to their pups, despite never having been exposed to acetophenone. These offspring exhibited shuddering more markedly in its presence compared to the descendants of mice that had gone through no such conditioning. A third generation of mice also inherited this reaction. The response can also be transmitted down from an acetone-sensitized mother mouse. Thus, the symptoms of exposure to a trauma may be expressed by many generations removed from that original trauma.

Parental Olfactory Experience Influences Behavior and Neural Structure in Subsequent Generations

Brian G Dias & Kerry J Ressler,
Nature Neuroscience 17,89–96(2014).

TOWARDS A GENETICS/EPIGENETICS
OF IRISHNESS

INTRODUCTION

"Living organisms consist of tiny microscopic units called cells. Human beings, for example, consist of an estimated 100 trillion cells. Each cell is the locus of complex chemical activity, called the metabolism, made up of hundreds of chemical reactions that occur simultaneously within it.

The metabolism is orchestrated by the cell's control center, the nucleus. The characteristic form of individual cells and whole organism (known as their 'phenotypes') results from this complex and interlocking chemical activity that is the metabolism.

Long thread-like bodies, known as chromosomes, constituted of a chemical called deoxyribonucleic acid, or DNA, and protein, control the metabolism and are found within the metabolism's control center, the nucleus.

The number of chromosomes in its nuclei are characteristic of a given species. Thus, human body cells contain 48 chromosomes. However, during the development of reproductive cells this number is halved to 24. In sexual reproduction, during fertilization, the 24 chromosomes of the male sperm cell pair with the 24 chromosomes of the female egg cell, thus re-establishing the characteristic number of chromosomes in human body cells, 48. The millions of cells that make up the human body all derive from repeated divisions that one fertilized egg cell, known as a zygote, and its derivatives. Thus, all nucleate cells contain 48 chromosomes, half deriving from the female parent and half from the male.

Each chromosomes is a linear sequence of chemical units called genes. Individual genes determine the synthesis of enzymes, proteins so specifically structured that each one of them facilitates the occurrence of a particular metabolic/chemical reaction in the cell. The metabolism refers to the sum total of such reactions.

In this way, the metabolism is controlled mainly by the genes of the nucleus, known collectively as the genotype. The complexity of this organization is indicated by the fact that the sum total of bits of genetic information contained by human reproductive cell chromosomes consists of approximately 20,000 protein-coding genes. The specific DNA complement of a given organism is referred to as its 'genetic code,' carried by the 'genome,' the full complement of chromosomes it shares with all other members of its species.

Thence, each organism has its own specific genotype, inherited from the reproductive cells of its parents. The precise nature of the metabolic activity orchestrated by its genetic code gives a species its characteristic form, or 'phenotype.'

This phenotype is amenable to slight variations mediated by the influence of the organism's environment. For example, identical twins have identical genotypes but not necessarily identical phenotypes as the environments *in which they are raised can never be absolutely identical.*

The effects of the environment on phenotype are mediated through proteins referred to as epigenes, the subject of much recent research, and which can modify the action of genes. Epigenes are also hereditable i.e. derived from parental reproductive cells.

It was believed until recently that genotypes could not be altered, still less permanently so, by the environment. However, the fact that it is now known that genes can be altered permanently by environmental factors and that such alterations are transmissible to the offspring of organisms (such as persons) so altered, is highly relevant to the following discussion.

For, traumatic stress has been found to be capable of inducing gene mutations and epigene alterations, both hereditable, with identifiable phenotypic and behavioral consequences, in generations far removed from the suffering that triggered such trauma."

TRAUMA AND EPIGENETICS

To access some current research findings and examples of epigenetic effects, the reader is encouraged to access the internet site: *Epigenetics–Wiki*. Here follow some summaries of material at this site that is relevant to this enquiry.

One fully-referenced study indicates that traumatic experiences, such as were suffered by victims of genocide and starvation, can produce fearful memories which are passed to future generations via epigenes.

Carried out as recently as 2013, it led to the discovery that mice could produce offspring which had an aversion to certain items which had been the source of negative experiences for their ancestors:

"For the study, author Brian Dias and co-author Kerry Ressler trained mice, using foot shocks, to fear an odor that resembles cherry blossoms. Later, they tested the extent to which the animals' offspring startled when exposed to the same smell. The younger generation had not even been conceived when their fathers underwent the training, and had never smelt the odor before the experiment.

The offspring of trained mice were 'able to detect and respond to far less amounts of odor...suggesting they are more sensitive' to it, Ressler told... of the findings published in the journal Nature Neuroscience. They did not react the same way to other odors, and compared to the offspring of non-trained mice, their reaction to the cherry blossom whiff was about 200 percent stronger, he said.

The scientists then looked at a gene, M71, which governs the functioning of an odour receptor in the nose that responds specifically to the cherry blossom smell. The gene, inherited through the sperm of trained mice, had undergone no change to its DNA encoding, the team found. But the gene did carry epigenetic marks that could alter its behavior and cause it to be 'expressed more' in descendants, said Dias. This in turn caused a physical change in the brains of the trained mice, their sons and grandsons, who all had a larger glomerulus—a section in the olfactory (smell) unit of the brain."

In other words, a behavioral reaction to a fear stimulus in one generation of mammals, namely mice, was related to phenotypic change (an enlarged glomerulus) and was repeated in successive generations who were not exposed to this stimulus, although the DNA of the latter generations remain unaltered. Trauma-induced Inherited epigenetic change was associated with inherited phenotypic characteristics.

But what could the transmission of such a characteristic in mice have to do with intergenerational transmission of phenotypic and behavioral characteristics in human beings? Answer: everything! For, there is absolutely no reason to believe that a similar mechanism would not operate in the case of intergenerational transmission by humans of behavioral responses to stress, since (it is necessary to note) the mechanism for intergenerational transmission of phenotypic characteristics and behavioral traits is the same for all mammals, human beings included.

In fact, another Wiki review that is worthwhile accessing, *Transgenerational epigenetics*, a parallel phenomenon involving human subjects is reported:

"In the Överkalix study, Marcus Pembrey and colleagues observed that the paternal (but not maternal) grandsons of Swedish men who were exposed during preadolescence to famine in the 19th century were less likely to die of cardiovascular

disease. If food was plentiful, then diabetes mortality in the grandchildren increased, suggesting that this was a transgenerational epigenetic inheritance. The opposite effect was observed for females—the paternal (but not maternal) granddaughters of women who experienced famine while in the womb (and therefore while their eggs were being formed) lived shorter lives on average."

In yet another review, *The Dutch Famine of 1944* (Wiki), the hereditability of stress-induced phenotypic traits in human beings is unambiguously indicated:

"This famine was close to unique as it took place in a modern, developed and literate country, albeit suffering under the privations of occupation and war...The well-documented experience has allowed scientists to measure the effects of famine on human health.

The Dutch Famine Birth Cohort Study, carried out by the departments of Clinical Epidemiology and Biostatistics, Gynecology and Obstetrics and Internal Medicine of the Academic Medical Centre in Amsterdam, in collaboration with the MRC Environmental Epidemiology Unit of the University of Southampton in Britain, found that the children of pregnant women exposed to famine were more susceptible to diabetes, obesity, cardiovascular disease, microalbuminuria and other health problems."

It could be remarked parenthetically here that the health profile of Irish women exposed to the Great Hunger, 1845-1847, and other Irish famines, and hence of their descendants, can hardly have been very different from that of these Dutch famine victims. To continue:

"Moreover, the children of the women who were pregnant during the famine were smaller, as expected. However, surprisingly, when these children grew up and had children those children were also smaller than average. These data suggested that the famine experienced by the mothers caused some kind of epigenetic changes that were passed down to the next generation. Subsequent academic research on the children who were affected in the second trimester of their mother's pregnancy, found an increased incidence of schizophrenia in these children. Also increased among them were the rates of schizotypal personality and neurological defects."

Can the elevated levels of schizophrenia in parts of the West of Ireland be likewise attributed to a genetically transmissible famine-induced effect? As is indicated by the above study, such a hypothesis could be verified by experimentation and observation using similar techniques!

To summarize, it has now been scientifically demonstrated beyond all doubt that human descendants of sufferers of behavioral or physiological symptoms induced by traumatic stress bequeath to their descendants, via the transmission of genetic/epigenetic material by sexual reproduction, the potential to exhibit the same symptoms.

Thence, given the elevated levels of intense

suffering and consequent traumatic stress endured by the Irish population throughout the period of colonial rule, including recent times, it would be indeed remarkable, if many individuals of the present Irish population did not exhibit the many stress-induced symptoms displayed by its ancestors. Indeed, we will see that diverse reports point to such a conclusion.

Does this mean that every single Irish man and woman is necessarily the "beneficiary" of a traumatically altered ancestral genome. Not necessarily!

What is being hypothesized here is that a significant mass of the present Irish population harbors such mutated genetic material and that this becomes reflected in the behavioral patterns, to be discussed later in this text, that give Irish society, viewed as a whole, its peculiarly individual cast, assessed in a general European context.

However, European and other minorities that have suffered cultural oppression (Maori, Bretons, Inuit, Scottish Gaels, et al.) may exhibit many symptoms of SCIS. In fact, SCIS is the provisional naming of a condition whose symptoms are detectable globally in traumatized communities and their descendants.

CULTURAL IMPLICATIONS OF EPIGENETICS

Experimental evidence continues to confirm the genetic and epigenetic origins of many psychiatric and somatic conditions and that, furthermore, environmental stresses can and do alter genes and epigenes that determine these conditions.

Thus, the "common-sense" assumption that multigenerational transmission of behavioral dysfunctionality is due solely to transgenerational cultural conditioning that is, in principle, reversible through appropriate behavior modification procedures and/or exposure to specific pedagogic routines is no longer tenable in all circumstances.

That is to say, the idea that children adopt behaviors of their parents *only and exclusively* through imitation, is superannuated in some cases by research that points unambiguously towards the involvement of genetic or epigenetic factors, or both, in multigenerational behavioral transmission.

Thence, culture/language rejection, for example, though it may be partially determined by cultural transmission, may also be an outcome of trauma-induced genetic/epigenetic change leading to neurological dysfunctioning.

So, the efficacy of mere administrative procedures and/or socio-linguistic engineering strategies in reversing negative perceptions of, e.g., the ancestral language of the colonized (or neo-colonized) subject may be questionable both in theory and in practice.

Thence, the question to be asked is this: does colonization-induced trauma runs deeper, and its effects become more "normalized" socially, than is allowed for in language revival methodologies developed to date?

Language re-acquisition strategies of the future must take into account the fact that deep-rooted aversion of many descendants of colonized peoples to re-possessing their ancestral languages may be partially rooted in an emotional, that is to say neurological, complex with a partial genetic/epigenetic basis.

PTSD: "OUR NATIONAL WALLPAPER"

"For decades after the Great Hunger scholars in Ireland rarely examined the catastrophe in terms of its enduring effect on the psychology... of the Irish people... It's possible that post-traumatic stress (PTSD) is such a constant in Northern Irish life now that it may go unnoticed. One of the hallmarks of post-traumatic stress is an intense foreboding about the future, even an inability to imagine one... Instead sufferers live their lives anticipating the next calamity–and it's no secret that the Irish, north and south, have lived like this in one way or another for decades. It's our national wallpaper really. In fact it goes much deeper into our national character..."

Cahir O'Doherty

Genetic/epigenetic and neurological studies link a complex of recognizably "Irish" character traits, what we term the Super-Colonized Irish Syndrome (SCIS), to heritable trauma-induced genetic/epigenetic mutation. Thence, we must consider specific hereditable trauma-induced conditions that may possibly contribute to the SCIS.

Post-traumatic stress disorder (PTSD), the most obvious synonym of SCIS, develops after the exposure of subjects to psychologically traumatic events, such as death threats or attacks on one's physical, sexual, or psychological integrity.

Among the symptoms of PTSD are re-experiencing the original trauma through flashbacks or nightmares, avoidance of trauma-associated stimuli, sleeping difficulties, depression, rage outbursts, guilt feeling, poor relationships with family and friends, substance abuse (so-called self-medication), hyper-vigilance, eating disorders, substance abuse, suicidal behavior, etc. They can cause significant impairment of social, occupational and emotional functioning.

Child abuse victims, massacre, disaster, torture and accident survivors, war veterans, even witnesses of trauma being inflicted on others, et al., are prone to suffer from PTSD. Symptoms of the condition often exceed the individual's ability to cope without psychiatric help.

An American war veteran with PTSD described how the condition affected his life:

"PTSD affected my life from the time I was 19, in ways that were not visible to everyone. I could not concentrate I could not sit still I could not sleep at night. I was very uncomfortable all the time. I felt like people wanted to get me all the time. I could not feel good about myself. I had no self-esteem and in order to be sociable I had to drink alcohol. I did not drink like other people. I drank to get drunk and I could act like normal people for a while, but then I would get very obnoxious and people did not want to be around me. I could not hold jobs because of the alcoholism, lateness to arrive at a job. I would forget where I was going or I started to feel as though I was losing my mind...I would have to pull over and cry and get my thoughts together and then try to get to work. No one would

believe what was wrong with me and I did not know either so my life was like a roller coaster. I would have bursts of rage and anger that I did not know what to do. I had so much anger that I was afraid I would kill someone..."

Just recently, May 2014, researchers at the University of California at Los Angeles (UCLA) extracted the DNA of 200 adults from several generations of 12 extended families who suffered PTSD symptoms after surviving the devastating 1988 earthquake in Armenia. In a genetic study of these families', the researchers found that persons who possessed specific variants of two genes were more likely to develop PTSD symptoms. Called TPH1 and TPH2, these genes control the production of serotonin, a brain chemical that regulates mood, sleep and alertness—all of which are disrupted in PTSD. *"We suspect that the gene variants produce less serotonin, predisposing these family members to PTSD after exposure to violence or disaster,"* said one of the researchers. *"Our next step will be to try and replicate the findings in a larger, more heterogeneous population."*

This is extraordinarily interesting.

Serotonin (5-hydroxytryptamine) is a chemical manufactured in the brain, whose levels in the body determine mood. Thus, a normal level of serotonin promotes feelings of happiness and well-being. But at times, the body becomes overly stressed and will begin to use higher levels of serotonin to compensate for being overwhelmed. Because of this, the body will not be able to produce more serotonin to replace the amount that was taken from the reserve. The body then suffers a recession, so to speak, which can lead to a mild to moderate case of depression. The lower the level of serotonin in the brain, the deeper is the depression.

Some symptoms of low serotonin levels bear comparison with those of PTSD; they are: difficulty focusing and concentrating, making "mountains out of molehills", chronic fatigue, appetite/sleep disturbance, eating disorders, low libido, low to no self-esteem, social withdrawal, depression, anxiety. Such low serotonin levels also adversely affect learning, ageing and memory.

Having inherited mutated genes from their once traumatized parents, the offspring of sufferers would thus have an innate tendency to express the same symptoms. And likewise, succeeding generations would be in receipt of mutated genes via the medium of sexual reproduction.

WHAT ABOUT THE IRISH?

Conditions favoring a marked incidence of PTSD, were abundant throughout Ireland in the 17th, 18th and 19th centuries, and in NE Ulster during the last 30 years of the 20th century. The survivors of the 17th century Cromwellian genocide, for example, survived experiences at least as traumatic as those experienced by 2nd World War concentration camp survivors who bequeathed PTSD to their descendants.

J. Lee and G. Moane, Irish psychologists, proposed in 1994[*] that centuries of English colonialism in Ireland relied on mechanisms of control, which included: physical coercion, sexual exploitation, economic exploitation, political exclusion, and control of ideology and culture. Specific traumatizing experiences for the colonized Irish, according to these researchers, include systematic treatment as an "inferior race" by the English, subjection to starvation (the Irish Famine) while vast quantities of foods were being exported, indiscriminate killings, land grabs, religious persecution, language and music censorship, and educational oppression.

They suggested that, for many individuals and families in "postcolonial Irish society", these mechanisms have left a deep psychological legacy of trauma along with consequences of: dependency; fear; ambivalence toward the colonizer; suppression of anger and rage; a sense of inferiority; self-hatred; loss of identity, horizontal violence, and vulnerability to psychological distress, all endemic to PTSD symptomatology.

Thence, It is entirely reasonable to hypothesize that Irish genocide survivors may have, likewise, transmitted traumatically altered hereditary material (DNA) to their offspring, provoking PTSD in the latter. And that the current population of Ireland still harbors such genes, with

---

[*]Lee, J. (1994). *The Irish Psyche*. Journal of Irish Psychology, 33, 1-20.
Moane, A. (1994). *Trauma and Cultural Oppression*. Journal of Irish Psychology, 35, 261-281.

the possible occurrence of psychological/ behavioral consequences for which they code.

The current extraordinarily high rate of mental disorders, including PTSD, among present-day children in post-conflict Northern Ireland is, once again, best explained in terms of such genetic transmissibility of the condition. Self-medication by substance abuse (alcohol, drugs), a frequent indicator of this condition, has reached, as we shall see, well-nigh epidemic proportions in Ireland, both North and South.

IS PTSD REALLY HERITABLE?

Earlier studies, conducted in the U.S.A. and Israel, on Jewish concentration camp survivors suffering from PTSD point, beyond any shadow of doubt, to the genetic transmissibility of this condition to their descendants. In one study, a single gene was identified as being a part of the body's stress-sensing system.

In response to stress, this system produces a hormone, cortisol, which is central to many of the body's biological responses to stress. This hormone is overactive in PTSD sufferers due to trauma-mediated chemical alteration (mutation) of the gene that determines its synthesis. Copies of this mutated gene are acquired by PTSD sufferer's offspring, via the route of sexual reproduction Thence, a potential for increased stress reactivity, PTSD, may exist in generations far removed from the original causal trauma.

In a study of child abuse victims, such altered genes were found only in victim genotypes, never in those of non-victims, and were associated with altered behavioral patterns. Hence, an environmental stress, sexual abuse and/or violence, has induced a gene mutation. This, in its turn, led to increased cortisol levels with consequent altered behavior patterns. Since such gene mutation is permanent, it is passed on to the descendants of the victim together with the altered stress activity for which it codes.

This possibility was confirmed by studies of the offspring of adult sufferers of PTSD who survived the 2nd World War Holocaust, child abuse victims, 9/11 and Vietnam, Iraq and Afghanistan war survivors, children in Northern Ireland: population groups where much higher than average incidences of PTSD have been detected. Information concerning all of these studies is readily accessible online.

The results of this research should not be seen as conflicting with the UCLA research described above; rather the occurrence of yet another hereditable mutated gene points towards the probable complexity of the genotypic, hence the body's, response to trauma.

Many other psychological states, especially schizophrenia, are now known to be hereditable. Joint genetic and neurological research is increasingly discovering that the basis of behavioral dysfunctions, previously identified as being purely "psychological", is now scientifically (thence much more usefully) described on the basis of interactions between the body's neurological apparatus and its genetic and epigenetic determinants.

"We (Irish) lost our history, and are still hurting. We're like a child that's been battered; we feel all the painful feelings but have lost contact with the memory. This leads to massive self-destruction, alcoholism, and drug addiction. That's what's wrong with us. We're suffering from post-traumatic stress disorder."

Does the above quote from Sinead O'Connor about her song, *Famine*, express a valid assumption? Does the genetic and consequent psychological residuum of the First Colonization of the Irish Mind, when compared with the effects of colonizations of other ethnic groups, make us Irish unique?

Or could it be that indigenous groups other than the Irish, whose ancestors suffered similar colonial trauma, exhibit SCIS-type behavioral traits? And, maybe, have histories from which we can glean some new and important knowledge about ourselves?

In fact, an abundant, growing and convincing literature shows that the behavioral phenomena associated with The First Colonization of the Irish mind were by no means unique in the annals of imperialist colonial expansion. Furthermore, comparison with the histories of other colonized indigenous peoples amplifies the probability that violent colonization left permanent genetically transmissible psychological scars on many of our ancestors, and thereby on some of us, their lineal descendants, whether in

Ireland itself or wherever the Irish diaspora exists.

Thomas Keneally, the Irish-Australian writer probably referred to a MGT/PTSD symptom when he wrote in his *The Great Shame*, that the Irish famine:

"...produced in the Irish themselves a certain amount of that survival shame which one encounters also in certain survivors of the Holocaust: the irrational but sharp shame of still standing when so many fell; the shame of having been rendered less than human by cataclysm."

The Multigenerational Trauma (MGT) concept, an apparent synonym of PTSD, is often used in this connection. It relates to the idea that descendants are affected by parents, grandparents, and extended family adults who were traumatized by war, genocide, sexual assault, torture, murder etc. MGT literature is reviewed in Coll, Freeman, et al. Many facts and ideas summarized below were sourced from that publication.

The symptoms of MGT/PTSD, are e.g. unprovoked outbursts of anger, bouts of depression, domestic violence, and self-medication through substance abuse. Being genetic in origin, successive generations of parents inadvertently "re-traumatize" their children. On-going oppression and poverty increase vulnerability to MGT, though drug and alcohol abuse—so-called self-medication—and other chronic mental health problems may persist regardless of socioeconomic level.

Growing evidence indicates that the signs and

symptoms of MGT/PTSD are prevalent over generations in all subject peoples traumatically colonized in recent historic times. Evidence of such recurrence emerged from the previously mentioned studies of World War 2 Holocaust survivor, refugee and other families around the world that are forced to deal with the multigenerational effects of genocide, mass killing and other collective violence. Long-term effects of such trauma have been defined as exaggerated and conflicted feelings of anxiety, panic and depression in descendants of traumatized generations.

Thus, traumatized Lakota Sioux in the U.S.A. were found to be still referencing the devastating effects of the brutal 1890 Wounded Knee massacre on their families 110 years later.

THE CUP THAT CHEERS?

In an online *Irish Independent* editorial (24/6/2014), as a response to a Health Research Board (HRB) 2013 report, attention was drawn to a phenomenon universally associated with the Irish condition, whether expressed in the homeland or abroad:

"It is probably true to say that as a people, the Irish have a strange, and probably dysfunctional, relationship with alcohol, or as it's more colloquially known, 'the drink.' We celebrate it in songs and writing and we have exported the Irish pub to the most remote outposts of civilisation. From baptism to burial, from sunny summer days to gloomy winter

evenings, from state occasions to the hard concrete of a city back alley, all, along with any other excuse, are occasions for us to break out the alcohol.

In fact, no celebration is considered complete without it. So we should not be terribly surprised that, apart from the estimated 20pc of the population who don't indulge, the rest of us are binge drinking our way towards alcohol dependence on an enormous scale. The two most worrying findings in a new report from the Health Research Board, which interviewed more than 6,000 people on Irish attitudes and consumption of alcohol, is that most of us are in denial about binge drinking."

That editorial extract was a response to a HRB study on Irish alcohol consumption in 2013. It found that 75% of all alcohol consumed in Ireland is drunk as part of binge-drinking sessions, that 150,000 people are "dependent drinkers" and more than 1.3 million people are "harmful drinkers". More than 30% of people interviewed said they had experienced some form of harm as a result of their own drinking. The drinking population spent over €50.6m on alcohol in the week prior to the study.

The World Health Organization (WHO) defines binge drinking as the consumption of the equivalent of three pints (or three glasses of wine) on a single occasion. Many Irish drinkers would regard three pints as the "warm-up" to some "serious" drinking.

However, Dr. Graham Love, chief executive of the HRB, said the report found that people underestimate what they drink by about 60%. If this is the case, then the situation is much worse than what has been presented in the report.

The linkage of substance, mainly alcohol, abuse is almost universally linked to the Irish condition. This isn't new: Spanish 17th and 18th century documents to which I have had access describe the notoriously insatiable thirst for wine of Irish vagabonds, male and female—refugees from the horrors of the Tudor Reconquest of Ireland and its sequels (ideal conditions for the development of PTSD)—on the highways of 17th century Spain.

Drunkenness reached such alarming levels in the cultural/linguistic watershed of pre-Great Famine Ireland that Father Theobald Matthew (b. 1790) was impelled to found a temperance movement that commenced with the foundation of the Cork Total Abstinence Society in 1838.

Under the auspices of this movement, up to 3 million people took a life-long pledge against the consumption of alcohol. Some still managed to stay within the "letter" of this pledge, by self-medicating on diethyl-ether, a pharmacologically much more dangerous chemical than alcohol. Father Matthew carried his campaign to the Irish and others in the U.S.A. where a statue to him stands today in Salem, Massachusetts, as well as on Dublin's O'Connell Street.

By the end of the century the influence of Father Matthew's temperance movement was on the wane, however, and alcoholism was once again becoming rife. To combat its ravages Fr. James Cullen, SJ, founded the Pioneer Total Abstinence Association of the Sacred Heart. By 1948, the PTAA claimed 360,000 members, known as Pioneers, distinguishable by their characteristic Sacred Heart membership badge, worn on the lapel.

The Association issued an appeal for funds from its website in April 2011 in an effort to prevent closure because of the organization's indebtedness. Its social influence has obviously waned in spectacular fashion.

To bring us a little more up to date, while alcohol consumption in countries such as the U.S. has recently declined by more than 1% over the turn of the century, in Ireland it increased by more than 39% (according to the World Health Organization Report, 2006). In fact, according to this report, the Republic of Ireland rose to fifth place in the WHO's global rankings for alcohol consumption.

Likewise, the latter source reported binge drinking to be dramatically on the rise in Ireland at that time, especially among young women. More recent media reports indicate that these trends are far from being reversed.

For example, online *RTÉ News* (11/5/14) reported that current WHO statistics show that Ireland now has the 2nd highest rate of binge drinking in the world. Furthermore, almost half (48.2%) of Ireland's drinkers are binge-drinkers, as against 24.5% of drinkers in the U.S.A. and a mere 6.2% in Italy, where alcohol is drunk to accompany food. This is the case in much of Southern Europe, where the habit of consuming alcohol simply to get drunk, as is all too often the case in

Ireland, is all but unknown[*].

Nor does substance abuse in Ireland pertain only to over-indulgence in alcohol. Illicit stupefacient usage has been rising steadily there and *RTÉ News* reported that Ireland had one of the highest rate of cocaine-related deaths in Europe in 2013 (11/5/2014). *The Irish Independent* (28/5/14) situates Ireland, with 70 drug deaths per million inhabitants, in third place in the European table of drug-related deaths.

Other studies consistently indicate higher alcohol use by Irish than other ethnic groups in the United States. They are reported as being the only such group there that has not adapted to U.S. drinking norms after several generations, adhering instead to the higher drinking norms prevalent in the mother country.

THE DEMON DRINK AND PTSD

Very significantly, recent research links alcohol and drug use directly to the occurrence of PTSD. Thus: One theory, the Self-Medication Theory, states that:

"...people with PTSD use substances as a way of reducing distress tied to particular PTSD symptoms. For example, alcohol may be used to reduce the extreme hyper-arousal symptoms that may be

---

[*]*The Guardian* 16/5/14.

sometimes associated with PTSD. Despite knowing that PTSD and drug and alcohol use problems co-occur quite regularly, research examining the reasons why this is the case is still in its earliest stages."

Other indicators of a significant presence of PTSD in the Irish population abound. Thus, Ireland has higher comparative rates of depression, domestic violence, post-traumatic stress, and child abuse compared to other countries in the European Union (WHO, 2006). Stress levels are hardly getting better when *RTE News* reports (29/6/14) that the number of murders rose by 36.4% over the previous 12-month period, according to the CSO statistics.

Closely related data show that Ireland "boasts" the second highest current (2013-14) suicide rate, after Lithuania, in Europe and, likewise, in the injury to, and abuse rates of, children.

Fellow EU members of the European periphery, subject to similar economic stresses as the Irish population, are found at the bottom of this list. So, economic stress per se obviously does not fully account for Ireland's horrific suicide and child abuse rates. To compound this abysmal picture, Irish female suicide, at 2.01 per 100,000 of population now (2014) ranks as the highest in Europe, with Greece coming in second.

---

*www.ptsd.about.com/od/selfmedication.htm

More such data could be adduced to further darken this highly negative picture of Irish mental health. Maybe Sinéad O'Connor got it right! Whence a national behavioral profile suffused with such negativity? And is such a profile shared with any other ethnic/indigenous cultures?

And, if so, what can we learn from such coincidences?

But, first of all, let us have a look at a possible pathological dimension of a characteristic of which we Irish are proud!

THE GIFT OF THE GAB

An endearing characteristic of many (invariably older, mostly of the pre-television generation) Irish people, according to visitors to Ireland to whom I have spoken, is the delight they take in conversation and banter. That trait that is referred to by the Irish as "the gift of the gab".

The more perceptive of these visitors note the frequent inability of their interlocutors to "stick to the point". Trying to find out something about the history of that ruined castle on the side of a hill, for example, they find themselves subject to a lengthy host of irrelevancies—snippets of family history, references to sporting events, opinions regarding the state of the nation, the relatives in Boston—and little, or nothing about the object of the now befuddled visitor's curiosity.

Starting out with the single-minded intention of tracking down that single elusive Lepus he now finds himself chasing wildly after all the hares on the mountain.

However, the latter's confusion is leavened occasionally by a wry turn of phrase, a little-known fact culled from that great Irish information resource, Pub-o-pedia, or an unexpected flight of fancy, clearly evidencing that James Joyce and the rest of his fellow scribes didn't take their talent for storytelling from the wind.

So, Irish tourism apparatchiks often tend to romanticize this conversational characteristic, some of them vaunting it as the basis of a literature that has acquired much traction, especially in the Anglophone world.

Eavesdropping on DART conversations, I note that such disjunctive dialogs are far from being confined to chats with tourists. In fact, it seems to me to be a conversational norm for many Irish people of all age groups. Could this chattiness bespeak anything sinister? Well, let us consider the following information culled from the U.S. online, *Slate*[*]:

"On the Aug. 24, 2001, Air Transat Flight 236 ran out of fuel en route from Toronto to Lisbon with 306 passengers aboard…Below stretched the Atlantic Ocean for hundreds of miles. As the interior lights flickered and oxygen masks dangled from the ceiling, weeping flight attendants instructed everyone to prepare for a crash landing into the sea. Then the pilot located a

---

[*]*Losing the Thread of Meaning*, K. Waldman, August 18 2014.

small military base in the Azores, and after 25 minutes of hell, plane touched down—violently, but without badly injuring anyone—to tears and applause…

Two years later, 15 of the men and women from the flight were asked to recount their experience. Researchers wanted to understand more about terror's fingerprints on the brain; the relationship between mnemonic habits and post-traumatic stress disorder; and what role clarity and vividness play in a given memory's power to haunt..

Half of the participants subjected to the air trauma developed PTSD. While most investigations of PTSD are limited by the diversity of experiences across test subjects, this one was unique in that it featured 'a group collectively threatened with imminent death.'

What varied among the accounts was the number of details that had nothing to do with the flight experience… Passengers with PTSD produced far more external details than those without… A survivor with PTSD was more likely to surround her non-emotional recollection with semantic data, repetition, and unrelated noise. The mnemonic motto for healthy participants, even those exposed to unimaginable trauma, more closely resembled 'just the facts, ma'am'.

Why should this be? The researchers note that people who score higher in neuroticism on personality tests also tend to thread their memories densely with external details.

Those with a weaker command over their remembering machinery may be at risk for PTSD, which is characterized by the chaotic bursting forth of past disturbances…"

In other words, on the basis of this account, PTSD sufferers would seem to be more apt to lose threads of meaning than non-sufferers.

Is this more circumstantial evidence that for the "Cahir O'Doherty/Sinéad O'Connor Theory of Irish Dysfunction?" When taken in conjunction with other PTSD symptoms, could this behavioural trait of many Irish people, "the gift of the gab", be considered as yet another indicator of PTSD frequency in the Irish population?

IRISH, SIOUX AND MAORI

The behavioral profiles of the Irish and the Lakota Sioux in the U.S.A. have been compared on the basis of their both these indigenous cultures having long and parallel histories of colonization*.

Both of these cultures currently struggle with extremely high rates of alcoholism and drug addiction; both have experienced systematic repression of their religions, languages, music and other traditional cultural practices. Both cultures are historically rural and have endured poverty, land loss, and experienced being forced into living situations and conditions against their will (e.g., relocation to reservations, cities; recall here that approximately

---

*Exploring Irish Multigenerational Trauma and Its Healing: Lessons from the Oglala Lakota (Sioux), Advances in Applied Sociology 2012. Vol.2, No.2, 95-101.

80% of the population of the Irish State were rural dwellers when it was founded in December 1922).

High rates of substance abuse, a key marker of MGT/PTSD, are found in all traumatically colonized indigenous peoples investigated, including the Irish and the Lakota Sioux.

A brief internet survey of such investigations indicates that this condition has much more than normal frequency among the New Zealand Maori, the Australian native peoples, the Canadian Inuit and other Native American indigenous peoples, in all of whose histories periods of intense and violent colonization figure.

Alcoholism and violence among Bretons, another European ethnic group that has suffered linguistic discrimination, have been related to what is described in an ethno-psychiatric study as the traumatic acculturation of that people by France.

In the case of one such colonized ethnic group, the Maori of New Zealand, many aspects of whose psychological and linguistic profile resembles that of the Irish population, trauma-induced genetic change has been hypothesized as a causal factor in that population's greater than average level of behavioral disorders.

The associate Maori Affairs minister, Tariana Turia, addressing a NZ Psychological Society Conference 2000, is recorded (*New Zealand Herald*, 31/8/2000) as expressing herself in terms that are bound to resonate with those familiar with Irish behavioral dysfunction.

Speaking to psychologists who frequently administer to Maori clients, she referred to a behavioral disorder referred to by the Maori as *mate*, and by New Zealand psychologists as Post-Colonial Traumatic Stress Disorder (PCTSD). The symptoms of this condition seem to be identical to those described for PTSD/SCIS.

According to Ms. Turia, Maori populations have a high frequency of individuals with a poor self-image, a tendency to self-belittle, to beat up parents/grandparents for speaking their mother tongue, of being unable to identify with the individual's tribe, of beating up spouses, children and siblings.

The latter is seen as an externalization of self-hatred, as evidenced by the number of Maori who are convicted of crimes of violence and the very high number of Maori women and children who are the victims of domestic violence.[*]

Other elements of *mate* are widespread alcoholism and predisposition to violent rage, two characteristics notionally associated with a particular mutated gene, the so-called "Warrior Gene", whose frequency is higher among the Maori than in white New Zealanders. Elevated 'Warrior Gene' levels are also found in other traumatically colonized peoples, such as the Canadian Inuit and the indigenous American peoples. I have yet to find a record of the frequency of this gene in the Irish population.

Ms. Turia continued:

---

[*]This rejection of the ancestral tongue as an expression of self-hatred, sense of inferiority and associated poor self-image, recalls 19th century—and some present-day—native speakers of Irish who deny a knowledge of their native tongue and the almost universal rejection of Irish Gaelic by Irish citizens.

*"The phenomenon of Post-Colonial Traumatic Stress Disorder and its effects now appears to be culturally integrated into the psyche and soul of Maori. It never used to be there. Indeed as Professor Anne Salmond has found, children were indulged and records of early contact show that violence towards children was... more uncommon than it was in Europe at the same period. Maori tribal commentators... have alluded to the cumulative generational effects of trauma or, as they put it, 'damage,' which has been passed down from the period of the Land Wars (1845–*1872, when 4000 Maori warriors fought against 18,000 British troops to retain their ancestral lands) *to the current generation of Maori..."*

For Maori, as indeed for all colonized indigenous people, identification of the trauma, as Post-Colonial Traumatic Stress Disorder (PCTSD) sites the issue in its proper historical, political and economic context. Ms. Turia concluded:

"The signs and symptoms of Post-Colonial Traumatic Stress Disorder (PCTSD) need further analysis and examination. My challenge would be for the... Maori psychologists amongst you, to lead the discourse on that analysis."

HAS SCIS A GENETIC BASIS?

Is the PCTSD one and the same as MGT/PTSD and the SCIS? On the basis of their almost identical symptom profiles, the answer has to be "most probably", though research would be needed to confirm such an hypothesis! Is the dysfunctional psychological panorama displayed by the SCIS victims more or less identical to the psychological profiles of other brutally colonized peoples that have so far been studied? Based on reports of such profiles, my answer to this question would be "yes", with a very high level of probability!'

So, to what extent is SCIS determined by the inherited genetic and epigenetic residues of the Irish colonial experience, without completely eliminating the possibility of ancillary cultural transmission of the condition?

One can envisage a series of fruitful researches addressed to this question in the areas of comparative history, genetics, epigenetics and neurobiology that should yield solid scientific information to replace the groundless guff, fruitless faux-romanticism, and magical thinking indulgence that bedevils so much past and present thought on the subject of Irishness and the Irish.

Transmission of distinct behavioral complexes characteristic of particular human societies from generation to generation was generally assumed until recently to be culturally mediated only. Offspring adopt, by imitation, the beliefs and mannerisms of their parents who, adapting themselves to the lowly status of colonized subjects, automatically pass on their tainted cultural heritage. And so on, down the line from generation to generation. The involvement of genetics, and still less, epigenetics in this cultural transmission was never considered.

However, the development of methodologies to advance our understanding of genetic-neurological interactions, and the findings they yield, have converted epigenetics and neuroscience into two of contemporary science's most exciting new frontiers.

Thus, we are now able to ask meaningfully: do genetically or epigenetically determined neurological factors predispose a significant part of the present Irish population to display the symptoms of SCIS, MGT, PTSD or, what has been defined in New Zealand as PCTSD? Such a research approach could lead to comprehensive definition of the neurological and genetic /epigenetic roots of SCIS.

To summarize, the strong circumstantial evidence now exists that genetic/epigenetic factors are at least implicated, if they are not fundamental determinants of the propensity to express symptoms of the SCIS, as earlier defined.

The fact that said behavioral characteristics are carried across oceans and generations provides further basis for such an hypothesis. However, until Irish subjects are experimentally tested for the genetic/epigenetic anomalies that are displayed by PTSD sufferers, this hypothesis, albeit a strong, scientifically valid one, must remain at the level of hypothesis.

The good news is that methodologies with which to expedite such investigations are becoming increasingly available. Hopefully they will provide us in the not too distant future with a key to a full understanding of the SCIS: a profile suffused with much negativity with its hypothetical roots firmly anchored in the complex traumatic effects of The First Colonization of the Irish Mind.

SUMMARY

Ethnic Greeks can define themselves as being of an unbroken cultural line that stretches back to Plato and Epicurus and beyond. A 21st century Irish person, however, can make no such claim, being of a broken culture that is still indelibly marked by the erasure of the language that configured that culture.

In this brief discussion, I have emphasized the key importance of the Irish Gaelic language, it being the most outstanding expression of indigenous or historic Irishness and the one living connection with Ireland's pre-colonial past. As such, the place of Gaelic in Irish society can be a litmus with which to gauge the cultural maturity of Irish society: by which is meant here the extent to which the Irish people have shed the cultural and psychological conditioning of their colonial past.

A brief summary of what is known about similarly brutalized indigenous societies in other parts of the world underlines the similarity of the cultural and psychopathological aftermath of the Irish historical experience to that experienced by such societies.

For example, the clinically verified propensity of the Irish to suffer substance abuse (mainly alcohol, but not exclusively so) accords with similar tendencies noted in the New Zealand Maori, North American indigenous peoples and the Canadian Inuit, peoples who all suffered violent colonization in recent historical times.

As such errant behaviors are passed on from generation to generation in all these groups, it was commonly assumed that they were culturally innate, deriving from imitation of the behavior and attitudes of colonized parents and, thus, repeated by generation after colonized generation.

However, the high frequency of multigenerational transmission of such psychopathological conditions as schizophrenia, for example, cannot be explained in such a facile way. The finding that the symptoms of the latter and of Post-Traumatic Stress Disorder (PTSD) are a consequence of trauma-induced genetic mutation of the victim's DNA and, thereby, hereditable, opened the whole gamut of trauma-induced symptoms to interpretation in terms of genetic and epigenetic transmission. Thence, a range of hereditable trauma-induced physical and psychological symptoms have been linked to detectable mutations present in the victim's DNA, along with epigenetic change, all inherited from the original victim of trauma.

This leads us to the experimentally verifiable (or falsifiable, in deference to Dr. Popper's rigorous criteria) hypothesis that the source of much errant Irish behavior lies, at least partially, in the chromosomes of the Irish population that contain genes—or associated epigenes—that mutated consequent on exposure to genocidal brutality and starvation over many past generations.

An ambiguous rejection of one's ancestral cultural and linguistic heritage is part and parcel of the behavioral complex of all brutally colonized peoples. Thence, it is also hypothesized here that the peculiar love-hate relationship of the Irish with their ancestral language, and their de facto rejection of it, far from being abnormal in a global context, is merely another symptom of a neo-colonized mindset they share with other indigenous peoples who have undergone a similar historical experience.

Only by fully understanding cultural colonization, in both its historical and biological dimensions, and recognizing its enduring effects, can we Irish begin to establish a firm basis for recovering intelligently parts of our ancestral heritage, above all that part encoded by our ancestral language, Irish Gaelic.

Likewise, such knowledge can help to better understand, and thence alleviate, socially disruptive symptoms of Ireland's colonial heritage. Genetics, epigenetics and neurology rather than speculative psychology and groundless theorizing may best steer us in that direction and help to finally clarify the conundrum of Irishness.

END

SOURCES

The following print and internet texts refer to, and expand on, some ideas and points raised regarding the various themes to which reference was made in this monograph.

Carrer, Philippe. *Ethnopsychiatrie en Bretagne.* Coop Breizh,2011.

Coll, K.M., Freeman B., Robertson P. et al. *Exploring Irish Multigenerational Trauma and Its Healing: Lessons from the Oglala Lakota (Sioux).* Advances in Applied Sociology. Vol.2, No.2, 95-101. 2012.

De hÍde, Dúghlas/Douglas Hyde. *Language, Lore and Lyrics: Essays and lectures by Douglas Hyde.* Ed. Breandán Ó Conaire. Irish Academic Press, Dublin ,1980.

Fernández Suárez, Yolanda. *Las "Hedge Schools" Irlandesas: Naturaleza, Etapas y Representación.* Tesis Doctoral. Departmento de Filología, Universidad de Burgos,2006.

Flynt, Larry, Eisenbach, David. *One Nation under Sex – How the Private Lives of Presidents, their First Ladies, and their Lovers Changed the Course of American History.* Palgrave MacMillan, 2011.

Hindley, Reg. *The Death of the Irish Language: A qualified obituary.* Routledge, London and New York. 1990.

Hurley, Richard. *Irish Church Architecture in the Era of Vatican II.* Dominican Publications, Dublin, 2011.

Kenealy, Thomas. *The Great Shame: And the Triumph of the Irish in the English-Speaking World.* Random

House Australia, 1999.

Kiberd, Declan. *Inventing Ireland: The Literature of the Modern Nation.* Vintage, London, 1996.

Leersen, Josep. *Mere Irish and Fíor-Ghael: Studies in the Idea of Irish Nationality, its Development and Literary Expression prior to the Nineteenth Century.* Cork University Press/Field Day, 1996.

Macedo, Donaldo, et al. *The Hegemony of English.* Paradigm Publishers, Boulder, Colorado, 2003.

Mac Síomóin, Tomás. *Ó Mhársa go Magla – Straitéis nua don Ghaeilge.* An Aimsir Óg–Paimfléad 6, Coiscéim, Baile Átha Cliath, 2006.

Martí, Felix, Ortega, Paul, et al. *Palabras y mundo – Informe sobre las lenguas del mundo.* Icaria editorial, Barcelona, 2006.

Memmi, Albert. *The Colonizer and the Colonized.* Beacon Press. Boston, 1957.

M. F. Ó Conchúir, Br. *Fothrach Folamh gan Áird.* Cló Iar-Chonnachta Teo., 1989.

Ó Ciosáin, Éamon. *Buried Alive – A reply to Reg Hindley's* The Death of the Irish Language. Dáil Uí Chadhain, 1991.

Ó Cuív, Brian. *Irish Dialects and Irish-Speaking Districts.* Institiúid Ardléinn Bhaile Átha Cliath, 1967.

Ó Giollagáin, Conchúr ed. *An Chonair Chaoch – An Mionteangachas sa Dátheangachas.* Leabhar Breac, 2014.

Unfirm Ground: A re-assessment of language policy in Ireland.

From Revivalist to Undertaker: New Developments in Ireland's 'First Language'.
Both from: Language Problems and Language Planning.

John Benjamin Publishing Co., 2014.

Ó Huallacháin, C. *The Irish and Irish: a sociolinguistic analysis of the relationship between a people and their language.* Dublin: Irish Franciscan Provincial Office,1994.

O'Toole, Padraig. *From Aran to Africa.* Nuascéalta, 2014.

Ó Tuathaigh, G. *Language, ideology and national identity* in *The Cambridge companion to modern Irish culture.* Cleary, E & Connolly, C (Eds.). Cambridge University Press, NY, 2005.

San Juan, Jr., E. *From the Masses to the Masses: Third World Literature and Revolution.* MEP Publications, Minneapolis U.S.A., 1994.

Terricabras, Josep-Maria, *Raons i Tòpics – Catalanisme i anticatalanism.* Edicions La Campana, Barcelona, 2001.

INTERNET

COLONIAL VOICES:
Ngũgĩ wa Thiong'o:
  timrdoc.wordpress.com/2011/02/02/ngugi-wa-thiongo-the-language-of

Memmi:
  www.scribd.com/doc/3047849

Fanon:
  books.google.es/books/about/The_Wretched_of_the_Earth

GAELTACHT SURVEY:
  Comprehensive Linguistic Study of the Use of Irish

*in the Gaeltacht: Principal Findings and
Recommendations, 2007:*
www.ahg.gov.ie/en/20YearStrategyfortheIrishLa
nguage/Publications/

www.drp.ie/essays/-in-tags/Joe-Mac-Donncha

GIROUX:
www.counterpunch.org/2014/30/an-interview-
with-henry-giroux-on

HEBREW:
en.Wikipedia.org/wiki/Hebrew_languages

IRISH LANGUAGE AND COLONIALISM:
www.arnold.classicauthors.net/Celtic
www.gaeilge.org/deanglicising.html

IRISH LANGUAGE: OFFICIAL DATA, ATTITUDE, LINE:
http://www.gaelport.com/mfai2014g

LATVIAN LANGUAGE:
*Language and Decolonization: A Latvian
Perspective,* Karl E. Jirgens (Lituanus: Lithuanian
Quarterly Journal of Arts and Sciences ,Volume
44, No.3 - Fall 1998.)
www.lituanus.org/1998/98_3_02.htm

LINGUISTIC THEORY:
es.wikipedia.org/wiki/Hipótesis_de_Sapir-Whorf

THE PSYCOLOGY OF COLONIALISM - IRELAND:
Father Matthew:
en.wikipedia.org/wiki/Father_Matthew

Lakota Sioux:
   http://dx.doi.org/10.4236/aasoci.2012.22013

Maori:
   www.nzherald.co.nz/nz/news/article.cfm?c_id=le
   objetid=149643

PTAA:
   en.wikipedia.org/wiki/Pioneer_Total_Abstinence
   _Association

Self-medication:
   www.ptsd.about.com/od/selfmedication.htm

Serotonin:
   http://www.ehow.com/how-
   does_4686190_serotonin-affect-mood.html

Stockholm Syndrome:
   en.wikipedia.org/wiki/Stockholm_syndrome
   www.irishcentral.com/opinion/cahirodoherty/Th
   e-trouble-with-the-cold peacein Northern Ireland

UCLA-PTSD:
   www.sciencedaily.com/releases/2012/04/1204020
   93509.htm
   http://gperiod2010africa.wikispaces.com/PTSD

APPENDIX I

CAN IRISH BE REVIVED?

Mainstream or "establishment" language revivalism, Government-sponsored or voluntary, has always been congruent with the maintenance of Irish as an official "show" language.

Thus, the "*A Chairde Gael*, I am very happy to be with you all here today..." mantra at the opening of political gatherings, and the "*A chara*" opening and "*Mise le Meas*" termination of official correspondence in English, instance examples of such mandatory tokenism.

Administrative terms such as An tUachtarán (The President), *An Taoiseach* (The Prime Minister), *An Tánaiste* (The Vice-Prime Minister), *An Dáil* (The Parliamentary Assembly), *A Chathaoirligh* (Chairman, vocative case) were imported holus bolus into mainstream English-language political discourse.

However, rooted in the antiquarianism of its 19th century progenitors, Irish "revivalism" never seriously contemplated strategies to replace Irish with English as the common vernacular of a modern state. Instead, by promoting Irish as a subaltern pastime language to be used mainly in limited diglossial contexts, official revivalism collaborates, with a State language policy that is, in effect, little more than a continuation of British linguistic strategy in Ireland. That is to say, by removing Irish from all important discourses, giving the status of an always optional extra, the language would, with time and common sense, gradually fizzle out.

Notable exceptions to such establishment revivalism emerged: for example, the group around the 1930s newspaper, *An tÉireannach*, Máirtín Ó Cadhain and his followers, *Gaeltacht* Civil Rights activists, et al. Éamon Ó Ciosáin's fascinating *An tÉireannach – Páipéar Sóisialach Gaeltachta* chronicles the fortunes of that newspaper and the activists who were associated with this radical effort. However, the *Gaeltacht*, decimated by emigration and economic decay, continued to decline.

Although limited, but important, successes were achieved by campaigns mounted initially in the 1970s by *Gaeltacht* and Irish language activists (e.g. the founding of *Údarás na Gaeltachta, Raidió na Gaeltachta, Gaelscoileanna*, a part-Irish-language television service, TG4, official European status for Irish, etc.) their impact was never sufficient to arrest the relentless decline of the language in areas where it was, or still is, spoken.

Paradoxically, the only area in Ireland in which a significant resurrection of communal Irish occurred, as a result of community activism, is outside the jurisdiction of the 26-county Irish State: the Shaw's Road area of Belfast, where a small urban *Gaeltacht* bucks, heroically, the overall linguistic trend.

In spite of such evidence, many revivalists in the past, even a dwindling few in the present have, or have had, the misconception that the State is, or could be, seriously committed to the restoration of Irish as a widely-spoken community language. All serious evidence shows that the State is committed to conserving Irish as a national symbol, full stop.

Thence, any serious attempt to rescue and revitalize Irish would have to be conceived, pioneered and engineered from within a historically/culturally aware section of civil society. Such a radical grouping does not appear to exist at present nor is it detectable on the immediate cultural horizons. This is not to assert that the potential for such a grouping does not exist!

However, serious Irish language activists need to be aware of tendencies rooted in the practice of their movement to date that have vitiated the possibility of successful language revival. Especially as the Super-Colonized Irish Syndrome (SCIS), as described in *The Broken Harp*, is a condition shared equally by all Irish people, whether Irish- or English-speaking.

Thus, under the heading *A Sociolinguistic Typology of the Colonised Mind in Aspirational Revivalism (as opposed to real regeneration)*, some such tendencies distinctly related to SCIS were listed by leading sociolinguist, Conchúr Ó Giollagáin (personal communication), as follows:

- A need for a symbolic comfort zone which descends into symbolising language to death.

- An adherence to a cultural viewpoint which resembles a virtual reality the more social practices become less rooted.

- An inclination to engage in avoidance strategies emanating from an inability to address real issues and challenges.

- A maladaptive tolerance of social dysfunction in the threatened culture related to an inability to think collectively and sociologically.

- A convenient social naivety among the elite class.

- A tolerance of leaders who will not lead.

- A fetishisation of the aesthetic and the past at the expense of the lived culture.

Any clear-minded person who has participated in Irish-language cultural or revivalist activity will readily recognize these SCIS symptoms and be able to cite examples of their expression at both individual and organizational levels within that ambience. Their negative effect on the ability of Irish language organizations to steer public opinion in a positive direction towards Irish is mirrored, however, by a corresponding set of SCIS symptoms in their target demographic.

Does it follow from this hypothesis that psychological decolonization of a significant part of the population is a necessary pre-condition of successful language recovery?

THE MAC DONNACHA SCENARIO

The sociolinguist, Joe Mac Donnacha, described the probable future of Irish in Post-*Gaeltacht* Ireland in the following terms:

"In discussing the prospects for the Irish language outside the Gaeltacht, it is reasonable to conclude that it will continue to exist into the far distant future in some form or other. It will exist in its written form in books, documents and libraries. It will exist in sound

and vision archives. And, for as long as the state deigns to support the language through the various levels of the education system, there will always be small groups who will be able to speak the language to a competent level of ability, and an even smaller number of individuals for whom Irish will be their primary language of choice in at least some aspects of their lives. This will be supported by a broader group of people who will have an aspirational level of interest and ability in the language. But this does not mean it will be a living language – at least not in any socio-linguistic sense."

This passage is an eerily accurate description of current Irish-language culture—the microworld of (mainly) "Pastime Irish" (PTI)—outside the *Gaeltachtaí* (Irish-speaking areas), but to a steadily increasing extent within the official *Gaeltacht* itself. It is a chilling thumbnail sketch of the likely future of the Irish language

But the death of the Gaeltacht does not necessarily mean the death of communal Irish, according to some language activists. A revival of the communal tongue will always be an option, they say. Other close at hand examples of revived-language cultures, but that no longer have a communal base, are those of the Manx of the Isle of Man and the Cornish of Cornwall.

I have heard it argued that the weakness of the latter limited, though otherwise admirable, initiatives is due—at least partly—to the fact that they lack the pedagogical resources and other materials needed to achieve their ultimate aim: resurrected communal languages.

In Ireland, on the other hand, and thanks to a century of language revival, a wealth of experience, academic research, archival sound and print records and learning materials would be available to future Irish revivalists should the *Gaeltacht* disappear. Thence, it is seriously held, the disappearance of the *Gaeltacht* as such need not necessarily inhibit the possibility of a resurrection of the language, even on a fully communal basis, should a future generation have the will and disposition to undertake such a project.

However, are we talking here about the recovery and development of a multifunctional living language, fully adapted to the communicative needs of a modern urban milieu? Or of a past-time folkloric/pastime language with limited communicative capacity?

The critical distinction between these two very distinct—and often opposed ways of imagining a "revived" language is seldom, if ever, discussed in Irish-language circles, most of whom seem in practice to have chosen—by unconscious choice rather than by commission—the folkloric/ pastime language option

However, based on the experience of the Irish language "revival", pastime and/or folkloric languages have an innately limited range of social application and, in the context of the life-span of languages, a probable inordinately short shelf life. Nevertheless, present-day mainstream revivalist culture reflects an emphasis on pastime language activity rather than on the more difficult task of devising an environment within which a modernized language could evolve.

The scant enthusiasm present-day *Gaeilgeoirí* (Irish

speakers) exhibit for Irish-language literature (see Appendix II) reflects the limiting nature of the current emphasis on pastime Irish. Yet, only through the medium of the written word can present-day and future Irish-speakers access to the full world view innate to the Irish language, to the extent that such is possible for strangers to the original Irish-speaking world of *Gaeltachtaí*, past and present.

Otherwise, the ability to speak Irish, or some simulacrum thereof, could well be interpreted as being a narrowly nationalistic desire to speak not-English, a language whose basic "value" resides in its unintelligibility to the Anglophone community.

Such a motivation for learning to speak some attenuated form of Irish, rather than Esperanto, say, while ignoring the cultural riches that the language offers, can hardly infuse learners with the sustained interest needed to surpass a limited grasp of the ability to self-express through Irish. And still less, with a desire to undertake the building of a community of such speakers!

Such deficient ancestral language learning motivation is far from being unique to the Irish milieu! A Breton source tells me that:

"Breton language enthusiasts do not read and are not interested in the past of the language. And they hate dialect divergence. They need a unified language. Children refuse to imitate the native-speaker's accent, as they deem it backward and peasant. So they speak their Breton as if it were French."

"What's the point?" he asks. *Touché?*

REVIVALIST CULTURE COP-OUT MYTHS

Magical thinking, propagated and cultivated by The Second Colonization of the Irish Mind, still manifests itself in unexpected places.

For example, why the lack of interest of a probable majority if Irish language supporters in the irrefutable evidence of the precipitous decline of Irish in the *Gaeltacht*? Such a reaction, or lack of it, seems to spring from an ingenuous optimism regarding language revival based on magical, thinking and a cavalier disregard for the grave difficulties inherent to such a project.

Thus, in a reaction to the news of Irish-language usage decline in the *Gaeltacht*, referred to earlier, I have heard such reactions as: "arrah, don't mind those damn statistics; they're only numbers! They were saying the same thing three centuries ago and the language is still being spoken".

Or, again: "didn't you see that article in the *Irish Times* reporting that Dublin yuppies are now speaking Irish "because it is cool to do so". Or another: "Pay no attention to that report; sure, it was written by enemies of the language."

And the latest fashionable cop-out myth: language death in the *Gaeltacht* is more than compensated for by cohorts of Irish speaking Gaelscoil graduates. The imaginations of some language revivalists even construct future *Gaeltachtaí* peopled by the descendants of Gaelscoil alumni who marry each other and propagate their own (Irish-speaking) kind...

Many "language fanatics[*]" allow themselves to become intoxicated by such exercises in self-deception.

Language revival "strategies" based on such scant regard for the conditions of language survival in the real contemporary world carry inbuilt self-destruct mechanisms.

Ceol agus craic, and the sundry expressions thereof are, of course, necessary recreational adjuncts to the cultures that all languages generate. However the repackaging of the entire language revival project as "Irish is Fun"—i.e. Irish as almost an exclusively pastime language, is seriously held by many Irish "enthusiasts" as being the only way to ensure the survival of the language.

Maybe they are not entirely wrong and that Pastime Irish is the only form in which Irish can survive into the future? However, arguably, such a survival can only have a limited shelf life, as suggested previously. Why?

Pastime Irish is, effectively, the synthetic *Géarla*, an Irish-English linguistic construct which, for reasons explained in the preceding essay, can only grow by

---

[*]All Irish-speakers, for the record, are either "eccentrics", "scholars", "enthusiasts" or "fanatics" in the general Irish Anglophone lexicon. Use of these terms, with whatever intent, creates a definite space between the Irish speaker and "normal" Irish society.

supplementing its vocabulary with English words and phrases. Thence, following the pattern set by all dying languages, this linguistic "halfway house" must eventually phase itself out altogether by transitioning into English proper, with the fig leaf of the occasional Gaelic phrase or pious invocation, maybe, for the sake of "ould decency".

No, Irish will survive as *Gaeilge*, the complete language, or not at all. But how can such a fundamental cultural/linguistic mutation be brought about in a super-colonized nation whose population is, at best, indifferent (and, at the worst, hostile) towards revival of the language? A nation whose will to recover its cultural, even national, independence is weak, if it exists at all.

This conundrum that has yet to be resolved by the Irish Revival Movement.

RE-GAELICIZATION: A REALISTIC OPTION?

Each of the three major colonizations described in *The Broken Harp* contributes to a behavioral profile of the population that Irish revivalists target in the hope that it will change its present attitude to Irish.

The present reality is that, for reasons dealt with in that essay, the culturally thrice-colonized Irish population neither sees nor feels any economic, personal, social or other conceivable benefit from sacrificing time and effort to the learning of Irish.

The ancestral tongue is not regarded as having sufficient cultural or commercial worth for this overwhelmingly Anglophone Irish population whose core values and general ethos now derive largely, and increasingly, from contemporary global consumerist/capitalist culture.

Furthermore, making reference here to the tenets of Social Psychology theory, people will generally tend to rationalize their present position on the social spectrum by seeking legitimate reasons for clinging to the status quo, any status quo, (economic, political, cultural, linguistic,etc.), whether they deem it to be advantageous to themselves or otherwise.

Add to that the probability that distaste for Irish speakers and their language, often masquerading as indifference towards them, may be none other than an aspect of the dissimulated self-hatred of the colonized subject, a symptom of a complex condition described in the preceding essay as the Super-Colonized Irish Syndrome (SCIS).

However, instead of learning from past failure and, above all, in the absence of a credibly realizable goal, the language revival project moves innocently on from one failed initiative to another, with accompanying wastes of time and resources.

In this Sisyphean never-ending task of re-Gaelicizing the Irish nation, the energy of many sincere and dedicated people, most of whom participate in the task on a voluntary basis, achieves little other than an agreeable modicum of cultural self-satisfaction for participants, often alloyed with a sense of frustration at the lack of any perceptible progress, sometimes leavened by a sense of community afforded by fellow believers.

The occasional mass protest, such as the *Dearg le Fearg* (Red with Rage) Protest that brought an estimated 10,000 Irish speakers and supporters to march on to the streets of Dublin on 15th February 2014, was admirable in the sense that it evidenced the collective frustration of a national minority denied its basic civil rights.

But, being outside the framework of a concerted long-term plan of action directed towards a discernable specifically-defined goal, it was an ultimately ineffectual gesture, albeit giving its participants an agreeable temporary sense of comradeship and collective purpose .

However, official State policy regarding Irish mutated since the 1970s from a revivalist to a heritage protection mode (From *Revivalist to Undertaker*, as Conchúr Ó Giollagáin entitles a recent paper), the outcome of such being copper-fastened by the 2012 *Gaeltacht* Act.

Thence, sporadic, and usually weak, protests against the failure of the State to fulfil its general constitutional obligations regarding the language will receive little more these days than evasive answers, polite acknowledgements, a deaf ear or the waste paper basket.

Nevertheless, in this distinctly unpromising milieu, an unregenerated language revival project trundles on, though the generations of our immediate past, and the vast majority of the present-day Irish people have, clearly voted for Irish with their feet (more appropriately, their mouths): THEY DIDN'T WANT TO SPEAK IRISH IN THE PAST and especially, given the powerful current hegemony of Anglophone Irishness, in both *Gaeltacht* and *Galltacht*, IT IS MOST UNLIKELY THAT THEY WILL WANT TO SPEAK IRISH IN THE FUTURE.

And this trenchantly negative attitude towards Irish, whether this vaguely-defined cultural product is presented to them as *Athbheochan na Gaeilge* (Irish Language Revival) or—the latest rabbit out of the revivalist hat—as a subaltern component of a notional bilingualism, the likes of which is not known to have ever functioned successfully anywhere, shows not the slightest chance of undergoing the sort of change language revivalists dream about.

So, it is past time to abandon the wasteful, futile and all but Sisyphean task of trying to convert the bulk of a thoroughly Anglophone population into Irish-speaking bilinguals, and to direct with desperate urgency—it may be already too late—all future resources and effort into more productive channels if the language is to have any hope of survival.

A CONCRETE OBJECTIVE?

Strategy options regarding achievement of a lasting Irish revival, are necessarily limited by the cultural reality of contemporary Irish society, as analyzed in *Strings of a Broken Harp*. However, options exist; their realization will depend totally on the creativity, energy of those willing to put their shoulders to the wheel.

A question from the floor! Does the approach suggested below imply the abandonment of the Éire Ghaelach (Irish-speaking Ireland) ideal of the Language Revival and placing all the energy and resources presently devoted to the diffuse "Irish For Everybody" (IFE), objective and more, at the disposal of a smaller community of committed Irish speakers?

Exactly!

What is advocated here is the replacement of a failed and, practically speaking, abandoned IFE approach by a coherent and realistic strategy that, by showing that Irish can be repossessed and revitalized at a community level, would focus a movement that currently lacks a realistic realizable goal.

Such a concrete focus is needed to replace the current listlessness of an Irish language movement that is vitiated by the same unrealistic broad, diffuse, unachieved—and unachievable—objectives that have informed its activities since its very beginnings.

Instead, let the long-term goal of Éire Ghaelach be situated in the context of a set of more limited practical goals achievable in the short to mid-term! The history of the Irish revival demonstrates clearly that while no magic formula for the re-Gaelicization of the Irish people exists, strategies directed to the achievement of more limited objectives have achieved some limited progress.

The development of the new Belfast *Gaeltacht* centered on *Cultúrlann Uí Fhiaich*, is an example. Likewise, the efforts to establish *Raidió na Gaeltachta* and

Teilifís na Gaeilge (now diluted to the English-dominant bilingual TG4) and the *Gaelscoileanna* movement.

The practical details involved in implementing the broad strategy proposed would, of course, need to be arrive at collectively by the organization or organizations concerned. But how, in the broadest terms, might this strategy be conceived?

NUTS AND BOLTS

Firstly, a short-term strategy to mobilize, within 10-15 years, the small national minority that is favorably disposed towards Irish and is willing to work for its' survival into a dedicated nucleus of fluent Irish speakers organized in a series of networks, or circles, of 6-20 members each, say, all linked loosely to a common administrative core.

These circles could be based on geographic areas, professions, trade unions, political and cultural organizations, schools, university faculties, sporting clubs, State departments, Gardaí, women's groups, emigrant groups, writer's circles, civil rights organizations, etc., anywhere and everywhere a group of persons with a genuine commitment to work for the establishment or survival of communal Irish exists.

The basis for the formation of such circles already exists in many *Gaeltacht* and some urban areas. An organized body would be needed to catalyze and direct their formation and coordinate their joint activities.

A condition common to these networks and their

constituent circles would be that their members develop a serious understanding of the value of the language and its relation to maintenance of a distinct Irish identity rooted in the tradition of the *Gaeltacht*, past and present, an appreciation of its present critical state and of the correspondingly urgent need for organized intelligent action if communal Irish is to have any future. Together with a commitment to work towards that end.

Thus, the initial phase of this campaign would need to have a strong educational component, with an emphasis on seminars, week-end schools, etc., dedicated to understanding SCIS and colonization/decolonization.

How should such circles organize themselves? What should they do to secure a future for Irish? If a basis for such circles really exists, how are their potential members to be identified? Let us take these questions in sequence.

One immediate and urgent objective requiring the cooperative effort of circles, particularly in urban areas, would be the establishment and management of Irish-language cultural centers—Belfast's Cultúrlann McAdam Ó Fiaich arts and cultural center serving as a possible model.

This Cultúrlann, established 1991, stands—with all its weaknesses—as a monument to what can be achieved by shrewd planning and dedicated cooperative effort.

Similar centers, serving as an initial activity focus for local circles, might be envisaged as eventually housing a range of cultural, educational and media activities to generate participation not only of circle members themselves, but of a wider, as yet uncommitted, group of attenders, e.g. Gaelscoil alumni, *Gaeltacht* immigrants et al.

As in the Belfast Cultúrlann, a bookstore and café/restaurant should be considered as an integral part of the cultural and social facilities of such centers.

Questions that arise here:

- To what extent would or should this community be virtual (i.e. integrated electronically) and to what extent physical (i.e. communal)?

- Should the surviving *Gaeltacht*, or native speakers in former *Gaeltacht* areas, be encouraged to play a vital, if not a leading, role in the project?

- What resources, and how, would need to be made available to convert English speakers into fluent Irish speakers with as near to native competency as is possible?

- To what extent should the State, and State assistance, be sought for the project?

- How can the human resources needed to mount such an ambitious program be assembled?

Clearly, the successful execution of such a project would require an enormous expenditure of resources and creative energy. But, if Irish is to survive as other than some folkloric heirloom, as a vehicle for *ceol agus craic*, no realistic alternative appears in sight!

The establishment of the circles/ nuclei proposed here, however, could only be regarded as a first step on a long time- and energy-consuming journey that could span generations.

THE VISION

Making the huge, and possibly unfounded, assumption that Irish language organizations and supporters would respond positively to the type of challenge described above, then what?

The culmination of this strategy, after some years of consolidation, would be the evolution of this pioneering core of linked networks into a substantial Irish-language minority within the State—20% of the population could be an ultimate goal.

This minority would need to develop the necessary levels of expertise, enterprise and political influence needed to enable it to construct the social, educational, technical and technological infrastructure required to ensure the continuity of its development as an irreplaceable, though linguistically independent, element of the life of a linguistically composite Irish nation.

So, the strategy and goal envisioned here is that of the stepwise creation, over many tears, of a strong, organized Irish-speaking bi- or multilingual minority in Ireland—connected mutually and with overseas' offshoots through electronic technology—whose internal activities are conducted exclusively through Irish and which is open to all modern discourses—scientific, political, sociological, literary, artistic, philosophical etc.—on condition that they be discussed and developed through Irish.

Just as such discourses are conducted through Icelandic in Iceland, with its population of 300,000!

IS THERE ANOTHER WAY?

Clearly, the successful execution of such a project would require an enormous expenditure of resources and creative energy. But, if Irish is to survive as other than some folkloric heirloom, as a vehicle for *ceol agus craic*, is there any realistic alternative?

In fact, the main alternative to such an admittedly radical, unprecedented, approach to the Irish language question suggested above is to stay on the same old track, continuing to witness, helplessly, the final demise of the *Gaeltacht*, and the complete disappearance in the near future of Irish as a community and domestic language.

Gaeilge easnamhach—would, doubtlessly, continue to be spoken with varying degrees of fluency within the gates of some schools and, socially, by a dwindling number of individual *Gaeilgeoirí* without. Scholars will continue to delve into the entrails of literature in Irish in an Anglophone neo-colony called Ireland. The very occasional Irish-language book published will be understood and celebrated by a tiny dedicated minority.

In short, what I could describe as "the Mac Donnacha scenario", as described by him in the earlier quoted excerpt from a recent article of his, is the certain outcome of the current directionless drift of Irish language activism.

That is, unless a realistic strategy directed towards the creation of a growing closely integrated Irish-language community from the scattered speakers of the language, along the general lines suggested above, is not formulated and implemented forthwith by a reinvigorated Irish language movement with a clear sense of mission.

No other language game seems to me to be worth the candle.

WHENCE THE TROOPS?

A key question is: are there enough committed and competent Irish speakers in the country to mount such a language recovery effort? Not all Irish speakers, possibly a majority of them, favor or are prepared to work for the survival of their own language!

Therefore, it would be critically important to identify from the beginning English speakers who would be genuinely concerned by the disappearance of Irish in order to persuade them of the necessity to acquire fluent Irish and actively participate in the effort to restore the language to full viability.

Most importantly, the life of the abovementioned circles and networks would have to be sufficiently rich and varied to attract a positive response from Anglophone cultural nationalists, the most probable source of recruits needed to ensure the viability of the project.

A crucial initial question to be asked: how are potential members of these proposed language networks, or circles, to be recognized and mobilized?

For such publicity to be generated, resources earmarked for Irish-language social activities would have to be diverted to a massive media campaign, to set out in stark realistic terms, and in plain English, the perilous state of the language, the historical and contemporary basis for such weakness, and the necessary steps that need to be taken to ensure its survival.

Thanks to the self-defeating tactic of hoodwinking the public—often by well-meaning revivalists—by withholding information that could galvanize potential activists, the latter are generally unaware that communal Irish is now on the brink of extinction. Still less are they aware that its fate depends on their own reaction to this fact.

Thence, a week of full-page advertisements, once again in plain English, in all national newspapers along with corresponding television and radio coverage, would go some way towards redressing this critical information inbalance. In the most unlikely event of resources for such an initiative being made available by official Gaeldom, the propagandistic creativity of the campaign's organizers would be tested.

Then, the question arises: what would recipients of this information do with their new-found knowledge? Where would they go and who would they contact if they choose to become fluent Irish speakers and to be mobilized to save and develop the language and its culture?

That question would have to be answered by all serious Irish language organizations. Would they have the will and capacity to cooperate to create the structures and resources needed to answer such an historical challenge?

Would they have the courage, imagination and creativity needed to abandon the failed revivalist strategies of the past and forge new strategies directed towards limited but real concrete goals?

Or, are these organizations so enamored of their traditional comfort zones, sectional interests and useless precedents that they would rather see, as I suspect, the strategy roughly outlined here as yet another pipe dream to threaten their comforts?

One is not encouraged by the polite hearing and cold shoulder Irish revivalists gave to Desmond Fennell when he presented them with his revolutionary *Iarchonnacht* proposal.

IS SUCH A REVIVAL POSSIBLE?

Where there is a will, there's a way, says the English proverb. But, in the real world, is there at present the slightest sign of such a development? Not to my knowledge! The human and physical capital—and, most of all, the spirit and will—needed for such an initiative seems to be almost totally lacking. On a Richter Scale of 0–10, I would define, making my most optimistic assessment, such willingness at present as hovering currently somewhere between 0.4 and 0.5.

Financial or administrative support from the Irish Government for a language restoration strategy that is plainly at variance with the Government's own plans, or absence thereof, other than conservation of a show language, is most unlikely to be forthcoming.

The level of competence, coordination, creativity and energy of the various present-day Irish language organizations—and their willingness to sink individual differences in order to cooperate in such a project—is problematic. The record to date is hardly encouraging.

Yet, the cooperation of existing language organization could be crucial to the success of the project, as outlined.

Of course, it is entirely conceivable that a vast majority of language supporters are happy enough to dedicate themselves to the preservation of Pastime Irish—an entirely different proposition to the development of a genuinely living "complete" language (which Pastime Irish or *Géarla* is not).

If the survival of Pastime Irish or Academic Irish is the sole raison d'être of such cultural activity, then I find it no less admirable than other cultural pursuits such as an interest in the music of various classical composers, 19th century Russian Literature, Esperanto, aboriginal wood carvings etc., etc. However, such "revivalists" should never be under the illusion that they are engaged in anything more than an engrossing minority cultural pastime.

The major obstacle to any serious public engagement

with a serious language revitalization project is the wide spectrum of attitudes towards Irish derived from SCIS, the etiology of which is dealt with in *The Broken Harp*, in the present Irish population, both Irish- and English-speaking.

A thoroughgoing psychological decolonization, impossible though it seems today, would be a necessary preliminary to, or concomitant of, any comprehensive effort to place Irish Gaelic on a seriously viable footing. As chickens don't precede eggs such decolonization would have to be an intrinsic part of any serious language restoration project.

For, without a clear historical perspective of how colonization affected, and continues to affect Irish behavior, replacement of the colonizer's language by the ancestral tongue makes little sense. And the more so especially when the imposed language is the language of the world's most powerful nation, with a vocation to be the sole universal medium of communication.

The latter basis of the "pragmatic" argument against the restoration of Irish evidences once again the "common sense" SCIS-view of fully colonized Irish subjects, who having fully assimilated the colonizer's myth concerning their own ancestral language and culture, can see no value whatsoever in forcing himself to repossess such useless baubles?

Before we consider the decolonization question, however, let us have a brief look at the human resources that might be available for recruitment to the language recovery project being described here!

In summary: whichever serious language restoration strategy is adopted, the formation of strong organized networks of Irish speakers and potential Irish speakers, circles, potential nuclei for an eventual strong Irish-speaking minority with the will and resources needed to ensure transgenerational transmission of Irish, would be needed to provide the necessary human infrastructure from which such a strategy could be directed.

Which is all very fine. But do potential members of the movement to be envisaged here exist in real life?

Maybe!

In spite of the demise of the *Gaeltacht*, there may still be a significant (albeit difficult to quantify) minority within the State, comprising native Irish-speakers, Irish-speakers of varying degrees of competency, and non-Irish speakers, who could be mobilized to learn and use Irish were it made *seriously* aware of the fact that communal Irish now teeters on the edge of extinction.

How big, roughly, is the minority referred to?

We really don't know! The number of daily users of Irish outside educational institutions was estimated some years ago to be 70,000, 10,000 of whom live in the present *Gaeltacht* areas (that is to say, 0.02% of the population as against the 20% who spoke it at the foundation of the State).

However some individuals register themselves as

Irish speakers on official census forms on the basis of knowing a few Irish greetings but are unable to conduct even a simple conversation in Irish. Official census data indicating that the number of Irish speakers in Ireland exceeds 1.5m, and is increasing, are not borne out by the evidence of one's ears in modern Ireland. Nevertheless, the belief that such a phantasy has some credence is not entirely dead.

All such figures relating to competence in Irish are suspect, and most probably grossly over-optimistic, given that we have no present way of assessing the competence of those who claim to be Irish speakers, even of those who live in "official" *Gaeltacht* districts.

Yet, elements of official "Gaeldom"—as reflected in a recent publication generously funded with public money—regard the inflated number of Irish speakers indicated by official census data as indicating that public use of the Irish language is on the rise, slowly, admittedly, but surely. The fact that US President Obama and the Queen of England delighted some ingenuous *Gaeilgeoirí* by using some Irish phrases during their Irish visits buttresses such a claim.

The prevalence of such magical thinking in Ireland has been referred to previously in this book. Believe in a thing, no matter how improbable, strongly enough—and wangle a few grants—and it will surely materialize! But, noting that such claims distract from the existence of a real problem, let us return to reality.

WHENCE THE FOOT-SOLDIERS?

We know for sure that Irish is still spoken and/or positively valued by a tiny minority within the State. But, there may be a real possibility that a potentially much larger minority, mainly of English-speakers, but with a genuine—albeit passive (at present)—concern for survival of the language exists.

The robust demand for places in *Gaelscoileanna*, for Irish courses for adults and for Irish learning materials and dictionaries tends to support this opinion though, perhaps, the significance of these tendencies should not be over-emphasized.

For, a necessary caveat here is that the motivation for the demand for Gaelscoil places may often have more to do with the excellence of the educational product being offered than any serious interest in creating young Irish speakers. Furthermore, the enthusiasm of adult learners—often encouraged by out-of-touch-with-reality revivalist propaganda—is often short-lived once the would-be Irish speaker realizes that mastery of the language, as of any language, entails many hours of dedicated plain hard work.

In the meantime, many who passively favor the restoration of Irish rest contentedly on their oars, believing that the dedicated work of *Gaelscoileanna* alone guarantees survival of the language into the foreseeable future. Such are the barren wastelands into which magical thinking carries away the true believer, the citizen given to temporary enthusiasms and the intellectually slipshod.

Non/or partial speakers of Irish, yet whose sense of Irish identity is still somehow bound to the existence per se of the language, need to understand that only active participation in a serious comprehensively organized language repossession project, with a clearly defined target and realistic intermediate goals, can avoid the complete disappearance of this prop to their Irishness.

This perception seems to me to be conspicuously absent at present not only among members of this latter group but even among the generality of Irish-speakers.

The upshot of these considerations is that a social space may exist—though the extent of it may be quite severely restricted initially—from which a well-constructed final effort perpetuate the Irish language could be launched.

Some crucial questions need to be reiterated. Firstly: can the Irish revivalist movement generate the energy, creative imagination and commitment to discover, cultivate and develop that space? And secondly: can revivalists propose a realizable credible concrete objective to convince the presently inert "favorably disposed" to engage itself in linguistic recovery?

Finally, is it possible for a super-colonized people like the Irish to advance in the direction of significant recovery of its original language without harnessing such an effort to a vigorous decolonization effort. In fact, is such linguistic recovery integral to decolonization and vice versa? Are they one and the same?

And, a final fundamental question, discussion of

which goes outside the ambit of this monograph: are cultural/ psychological decolonization and participation in the global neoliberal economy and its attendant culture compatible?

IS DECOLONIZATION POSSIBLE?

The basic sine qua non of colonized subject decolonization is that deep historical knowledge whose very possession initiates elimination of psychological accommodation to the SCIS of contemporary Irishness. It must initially incorporate a deeply-felt discomfort at the realization or consciousness, that such psychological bondage still exists and is culturally determinative.

True full independence from foreign cultural occupation never occurred to any significant extent in any part of Ireland. Real decolonization, implies complete and total elimination of Irish psychological subservience, as encoded for by the colonizer's language, English. It has yet to be seriously undertaken, almost a century after the physical departure of the colonizer.

Indigenous decolonization is complex and not advanced by half-measures, as both Albert Memmi and Franz Fanon were at pains to point out. It must incorporate physical, psychological, emotional and spiritual strategies as each of these human registers are affected directly by colonialism. True decolonization can be achieved only when all of these components have been addressed or met in some effective manner.

Without a deep empathic understanding of Irish history from the perspective of the colonized subject and, hence, of the colonizing process itself, as it played itself out in Ireland, and the mechanisms of its enduring negative effects on the Irish population, described earlier in this book, the widespread sense of urgency and active commitment needed to re-establish Irish as a widely spoken language in Ireland could hardly develop.

This re-education process commences when the colonized subject realizes through study and experience that he is, in fact, colonized, what this entails, and then assimilates the truly traumatic history of his people into his very being.

In the process of this painful self-exploration, his mythical or "lower-status" self (Fanon's "colonizer's myth", or national stereotype, internalized by colonized subjects) dissolves and the liberated subject is freed to embrace again his native culture, language and religion.

Wole Soyinka (b. 1934), the Nigerian poet, writer, cultural activist and Nobel Prize winner (1984), expressed the nature of that liberating moment in the passage of his, previously quoted in page 105:

It involves, very simply, the conscious activity of recovering what has been hidden, lost, repressed, denigrated, or indeed simply denied by ourselves etc., etc.

Unless the rigors of the demythologization process described by Soyinka are undergone, the colonized Irish subject is destined to remain a prisoner of his "national" self, as mythologized by the English colonizer.

The good SCIS-affected citizen may choose to learn the *cúpla focal*, of course, and without going too far over the top, sometimes use them—sparingly, though, no fanaticism there—under those rare diglossial circumstances whose occurrence are becoming rarer still in the present-day Irish cultural province of the British Isles. But that is about as far as the "Irish Revival", as construed by state officialdom, goes at present. And can go!

But, unless a significant section of the population is impelled to question and then shed this condition of neo-colonized Irishness, all the socio-linguistic engineering in the world will never conserve, let alone create, an Irish-speaking community.

Or, to put a more positive spin on this bleak forecast, a socio-linguistic engineering project such as is proposed here can only work after the SCIS has been effectively routed from the minds of a community-sized group of citizens.

But has a like linguistic project ever been successfully, or otherwise, attempted?

Or succeeded?

Anywhere?

At any time?

WHAT ABOUT HEBREW, THEN?

The rebirth of Hebrew is cited by many Irish revivalists as the case of a seemingly dead language being successfully revived and adapted to modern living.

It is time to lay that myth to rest.

For, the cases of Hebrew and Irish revival are

about as comparable as chalk and cheese. The main problems to be solved by Hebrew revivalists were qualitatively different from those facing their counterparts in Ireland.

Jewish colonists in Palestine, the later Israel, needed a common tongue since the Jewish colonists living there were of diverse linguistic origins. Most early colonists were of Middle and Eastern European origin and spoke Yiddish, a German dialect with Hebrew loan words, or standard German, *Hochdeutsch*, itself. The second largest group, the Sephardim, descendants of Jews deported from medieval Spain and inhabiting a number of Mediterranean and Middle Eastern countries, and parts of Latin America, spoke Judeo-Spanish, a dialect of medieval Spanish. Some spoke Arabic. Others spoke a variety of European, Slavic and Semitic tongues.

But Hebrew, the common liturgical language of Jews everywhere, was an obvious candidate— among the less favored ones, including Yiddish and English—when the pressing practical need for a common day to day language had to be decided upon.

This choice had been already made spontaneously on the ground, so to speak, prior to any official promotion of the Hebrew. Thanks to the Hebrew-based education of a significant number of immigrants in Jewish schools, the *Yeshiva*, knowledge of basic Hebrew grammar was common among the Jewish immigrants to Palestine. So, not surprisingly, the language had been the *lingua franca* of Jewish merchants, of diverse linguistic backgrounds, established in Palestine since the first half of the 19th century.

However, unlike those immigrants to Palestine from the Jewish Diaspora, most Irish people have had a common spoken language, English, since the end of the first half of the 19th century.

Thence, Irish revivalists can never be in a position to appeal to a linguistic need comparable to that of the need of the Jews of Palestine/Israel for a common language. The primacy of a recognizably Hibernian-accented form of the English language, with its characteristic idiomatic idiosyncrasies, constitutes the essential linguistic dimension of post-Gaelic Irishness.

CAN EXTINCT LANGUAGES BE REVIVED?

Attempts to resuscitate extinct native indigenous languages in North America are worth noting. For example, the Yurok language of California, whose last native speakers died towards the end of the last century—according to archival records—was revived and is now taught in four public high schools in Eureka, Northern California, and two elementary schools, one of which offers an immersion course in the language (*New York Times*, 13/4/2014).

However, it is impossible to gauge the efficacy or the aims of this revival from this article. Questions that would need to be asked from our perspective, and that is unanswered in the cited article, are:

To what extent has the Yurok language become again the communal language of a significant part of the Yurok community?

- Is it transmitted again from elders to their young?

- Can it be a whole/complete language usable in modern contemporary contexts or is it deficient in the essential registers needed to have Yurok defined as such?

- Does the bilingual ambience in which it has been revived define this subaltern tongue as a "folkloric", "ritualistic" or "pastime" language whose use is limited to certain well circumscribed traditional or cultural contexts?

If the answer to the last question is affirmative (as I suspect it is), Yurok would be categorized, along with other "revived" indigenous languages (as distinct from still living languages such as Nahuatl, Navajo and Cree) in California, and North America in general, whose use seems to be confined to certain resuscitated traditional ceremonies, often of a religious nature!

In fact, the status of Yurok may very well have certain similarities to that of much Irish spoken outside the *Gaeltacht* and, increasingly, inside the *Gaeltacht* itself, whose use is confined to certain defined educational and recreational contexts?

Or, indeed, the status of Yurok may also be like that of Manx and Cornish, both Celtic languages that have a number of individual fluent speaker-learners, although neither has had communities of native speakers for some considerable time: centuries in the case of Cornish, a close relative of Breton and Welsh and less than one century in the case of Manx, a sister language of Irish and Scottish Gaelic!

In fact, by the time the speech of the last verified native speakers of Manx was recorded by the Irish Folklore Commission in the 1930s, the language had ceased to be a community language. This was reflected in the level of conversational fluency— reminiscent of that encountered in recordings made by the Irish Folklore Commission of the speech of the last native Irish-speakers of Tyrone—of these last speakers of Manx.

Thence, it is to the credit of their proponents that both Manx and Cornish now boast a growing number of learners who speak these languages with varying degrees of proficiency. But, given the severely circumscribed cultural space that Manx and Cornish now occupy in the Isle of Man and Cornwall, one would have to refer to these Celtic languages— for the time being at least—as being folkloric.

Is relegation to the folkloric sphere—and thence to a merely ceremonial communal status—the inevitable fate of any "revived" language that finds itself yoked in a bilingual context to an immensely more powerful language? The almost universal loss of native Irish, for example, and the simultaneous overwhelming linguistic hegemony of English in Ireland answers this question, perhaps.

Such language loss has certain inevitable consequences.

Linguistic domination entails cultural supremacy, as Ngugi Wa Thiong'o has pointed out. Those who control meanings and conventions of discourse are also able to promote their world view, norms, values and interests. Those who are denied the right to use their language in all forms of social life are hindered in expressing themselves, in shaping reality, in drawing attention to their needs, and in commanding support from others.

However, the unique Israeli experience suggests that, given the requisite tenacity of will—and highly specific historical circumstances—such a fate need not necessarily be always so. (The singularity of the Israeli linguistic experience, described previously, is continued in the following section.)

We saw that this Hebrew revival sprang from the pragmatic need of a linguistically diverse population for a common tongue.

Irish revivalism, on the other hand, was birthed in an overwhelmingly Anglophone society by the anti-colonialist notion of refurbishing a cultural connection with the historic Irish nation. Thence, the existence of the language provided a fundamental ideological justification for breaking the connection with England and establishing a notionally decolonized independent Irish state.

Once that latter connection was partially broken, however, whatever head of steam was left in the language revival project gradually dissipated. The superficial trappings of political independence seemingly satisfied most leaders of the new Irish State. The decolonizing cultural and social changes envisaged by Pearse and Connolly, the 1916 Rising leaders, were never seriously on their agenda.

Thus, the pre-revolutionary colonial ethos, hardly missing a beat, quickly reasserted itself after the announcement of this notional independence.

Ironically, almost a century after 1916, advocates for the decolonization of Ireland, economically, socially, culturally and linguistically, are lone voices in the *"Sacsa Nua darbh ainm Éire"* (a new England called Ireland), Post-Gaelic Ireland, a component of the British Isles (and never more appropriately named).

"A New England called Ireland": so modern Ireland was visualized in the far-seeing Fearflatha Ó Gnímh's poetic prophecy, written at the beginning of the 17th century, probably after the fateful Battle of Kinsale in 1601 sealed the fate of the Gaelic Irish nation.

And the Irish language has largely become just another folkloric reminder of a time when the poet's *Sacsa Nua* had yet to be born.

Could things have been different? Could things still be different?

Posed now In Ó Gnímh's *Sacsa Nua* of 2014, when the names and, more particularly, the ideals of the 1916 revolutionary leaders, Pádraig Pearse and James Connolly, are on the point of being written out of the dominant Irish history narrative, these questions have an irremediably subversive ring to them!

LESSONS FROM HEBREW?

Drawing attention to fundamental qualitative differences between the Hebrew and Irish revivals, as described above, however, was far from suggesting that a resurgent Irish-language movement might have had nothing to learn from the Israeli linguistic experience.

For example, the pedagogical techniques and technology employed by Israel to convert speakers of diverse tongues, many with little or no knowledge of Hebrew, into fluent speakers of that language within a short space of time, capable of living and learning in the sophisticated and advanced technological culture that is Israel through the medium of Hebrew, are worthy of study.

That language has indeed come a long way since indeed Eliezer Ben-Yehuda (1858–1922), campaigned for the lay use of Hebrew in the then Palestine that predated Israel.

The latter considerations invite yet another important reflection. Most Israelis are bilingual, if not multilingual, and knowledge of English in Israel is widespread. These linguistic abilities are seen as being, pragmatically, the gateway not only to the technological and scientific knowledge that the modern nation-state deems essential to its survival but to the whole gamut of human experience.

Yet, instead of relegating Hebrew to a subaltern status in relation to English (as happened to Irish in Ireland), Israelis import from English and all other developed languages the riches of modern intellectual and scientific discourse into Hebrew, which is thereby enriched and made adequate to express almost all significant nuances of the modern condition.*

In this context, it amounts to a redundancy to say that as long as the protagonists of Irish are content, or forced, to allow the language to confine itself mainly to the antiquarian and entertainment (*craic agus ceol*) slots, the language can never, and will never, become the principal medium of communication of an organic modern community with a future. That is, a community in which scientific and technological thinking plays a preponderant part in, and thoroughly permeates, a significant part of its intellectual life.

Such a community, to avoid misunderstanding, can never exclude those social, esthetic and moral concerns that cement any viable civilized society. But the days of languages whose scope to a limited range of cultural expression, being largely content to relive, and bask in, the reflected glory of their real and invented pasts, are well and truly numbered.

THE LIMITATIONS OF FOLKLORIC LANGUAGES

The unique referential universe of a any given language is shaped by the history, art and traditions of the users of that language and informs every aspect of life of its shared life. It is possession of that unrepeatable world view that gives each distinct ethnic group its

---

*The author's positive evaluation of the revival of Hebrew in Israel in no way implies his support for the latter nation's brutal attempt to eliminate the possibility of a just shared future with the dispossessed Palestinian people.

unique understanding of life and its own unique creative possibilities.

The breadth of the shared life of speakers of a language determines the boundaries of its referential universe. Where that shared life does not encompass modern science, technology, philosophy, for example, the language cannot expand to describe these areas of lived human existence.

Such a language could be referred to as being "folkloric", i.e. as having a referential universe located essentially in past custom and being no longer adequate to describing the constantly changing universe in which its speakers now find themselves.

In practice, the main referential universe of speakers of *an teanga easnamhach*, the current form of most spoken Irish, on the other hand, is that of the English language, along with the weight of cultural and social baggage inherent to that language. Thus, there can be no significant difference between the culture of English speakers in contemporary Ireland and that of *teanga easnamhach* speakers other than that the latter may have the hypothetical possibility of broadening their knowledge of Irish language culture and, thence, of adding, both qualitatively and quantitatively, to their referential universe.

However humanly enriching that latter experience may be, given the absence of an integral community-based Irish-language culture that embraces modern life in all its varied aspects, such an option can never answer fully to that broad spectrum of needs that define the being of advanced 21st century societies. A modern monolingual Irish-language culture cannot be, given the limited cultural niche now occupied by that language, a realistic option at this time.

To rescue the language from its folkloric state, its speakers would need to be fully involved in all aspects of the referential universe common to the more developed languages—that is to say English, usually, in the case of Ireland. Like Hebrew speakers vis-à-vis Hebrew, they would have to be committed to incorporating insights garnered from English (or French, Russian, Japanese, Spanish, etc.) into their spoken and written Irish.

The present ongoing Quixotic task of keeping scientific, medical and technical vocabulary of Irish abreast of that of English is precisely that, Quixotic, in the sense that the culture and worlds into which this vocabulary could be integrated do not, in fact, exist, and seem increasingly unlikely to ever materialize.

Without the development of a societal arrangement within which the necessary renaissance of Irish and the Gaelicization of the corresponding areas of research could occur simultaneously, those specialized dictionaries amount to, and most regrettably, elegantly well-dressed corpses patiently awaiting the trumpet call of an increasingly improbable resurrection. Use of the term "resurrection" in this context is fanciful, however, implying as it does previous live situations that never existed in reality…

APPENDIX II

GAELIC LITERARY CULTURE: AN UNSUNG DEATH?

"Suppose he (the colonized), has learned to manage his language to the point of re-creating it in written works; for whom shall he write, for what public? If he persists in writing his language, he forces himself to speak before an audience of deaf men. Most of the people are uncultured and do not read any language, while the bourgeoisie and scholars listen only to that of the colonizer. Only one natural solution is left; to write in the colonizer's language..."

Albert Memmi

The vitality of its literary culture is a commonly accepted index of the very vitality of a modern language, whose development is both reflected in, and configured by, the printed word. Conversely, the shelf life of a modern language that lacks a vigorous literary culture is apt to be brief, relative to that of languages well served by the printed word, as witness the terminal decadence of most of Europe's minority languages (including Irish and Scottish Gaelic).

In short, in the context of language survival, the literary culture of a language is no optional extra.

However, Irish-language literary culture is dying quietly on the vine, just as the spoken language loses its flexibility and ability to engage adequately and creatively with the changing contours and breadth of modern urban living. These two phenomena are far from being unrelated, I suggest.

Significantly, Irish-speakers are no longer served by a printed newspaper, even a weekly one. The plug was pulled recently on the few printed magazines, bar one (at the time of writing), that served readers of Irish. This act of cultural vandalism—the phrase is hardly excessive—failed, unsurprisingly, to generate any protest of which I am aware from any significant body of Irish speakers.

Foras na Gaeilge, the body responsible for the promotion of the Irish language throughout Ireland, is commissioned to deploy State funding to that stated end. Did a decision by Foras in 2014 to replace printed media in Irish with some equivalent online services follow a wide-ranging consultative process involving Irish-language readers? Did it take into account the age profile of the latter? Or how many of these readers have access to computers and are computer-literate, for example? Not that many, I would guess!

The increased online presence of Irish is, of course, a positive and necessary step in the promotion of Irish. No argument there! But readers of Irish, particularly those who have yet to become computer literate, are hardly likely to regard it as an unqualified boon when this advance is made at the expense of the long-established, and still vitally necessary, Irish-language print media.

For, although electronic communications media and e-books are gradually displacing their print forbears globally, the latter—to hazard a not totally uninformed guess—are still probably preferred by most serious readers of Irish.

In spite of the rapid advance of electronic media in recent years, and a corresponding worldwide decline in the vitality of print media, the Gutenberg Revolution has still to run its full course. And not only in Ireland! The speakers of every official EU language, except Irish, have at least one daily printed newspaper. Ditto for every major U.S. city! Ireland offers a choice of daily and weekly printed newspapers in English.

The Irish language, however, has neither a daily nor a weekly, nor any print newspaper whatsoever. And now, by recent fiat of *Foras na Gaeilge*, funding to maintain even the few monthly Irish-language magazines that survive has also been cut.

In this somewhat arid literary landscape, instead of vigorously promoting the written word in Irish, the Foras seems—incomprehensibly—to interpret the phrase "promotion of Irish", as a mandate to destroy a key part of the Irish-language literary culture infrastructure. As if its covert mission was to promote linguicide rather than language restoration. Is use of such an expression mere hyperbole?

Not really! For, the effect of this policy effectively annihilates most of the space available until recently to young writers and journalists to hone their literary and communicational skills through the medium of Irish. The knock-on effect of such a vacuum can only be to gravely impede the development of Irish as a modern and flexible literary and general communications medium. Thence, it is a vacuum that can only have the gravest implications for the very survival of the language itself as a vehicle to facilitate and advance modern discourse.

So, how fares the Irish language in book format? As the Irish–English hybrid, *Géarla,* rather than *Gaeilge* (the complete language in which the literary language is couched), predominates in the "Irish-language community", most members of the latter are unable to read Irish without constant reference to a dictionary. Unsurprisingly, they do not buy books they cannot read. They buy and read books in English, which offer them no such difficulty.

Thence, it is hardly surprising that an integral Irish-language literary culture is dying a largely unnoticed death. By "integral literary culture" is meant here the entire literary enterprise, extending from writer to reader, involving agents, artists, publishers, publicists, distributors, a corps of suitably experienced and competent critics, et al. Such an industry does not exist through the medium of Irish other than in a highly attenuated form.

The recent appointment of a fulltime book distributor by *Foras na Gaeilge* is a step in the right direction. But it is an infinitesimally tiny drop in the ocean compared with the massive investment needed to construct a viable Irish-language literary culture. Furthermore, for reasons just mentioned, such an investment would make little sense in the absence of substantial investment in educational policies directed at greatly upgrading the general level of learned Irish from *Géarla* to *Gaeilge* and, thus, promoting genuine Irish-language literacy.

In spite of this unpropitious situation, and unknown to the country at large, even to most Irish speakers for reasons just described, work of international caliber in all literary genres is still being produced by Irish-language writers and poets. Among the many other constraints the latter have to contend with, both the almost complete absence of informed critical response to their work, together with media (including Irish-language media) unwillingness to give it any publicity whatsoever, are outstanding.

The main responsibility for the dearth of criticism of current literary production must be laid at the doors of Third-Level Irish departments that hone their student's critical skills on folkloric texts rather than on recent writing (as students from these departments have informed me) and to whom modern innovative writing in Irish appears to be anathema. Graduates in Irish to whom I have spoken claim not to have been pressured ever to read a single line written by Máirtín Ó Cadhain, arguably the finest Irish-language fiction writer ever. Imagine an English-language graduate never having to read a line of Shakespeare, a Spanish literature graduate who had not read Cervantes!

Thence, to summarize, the major constraint on the development of Irish-language literary culture resides in the non-existence of a viable market for its products. *Géarla* speakers find written *Gaeilge* to be too difficult. The unwillingness of Government and decision makers in the educational and Irish-language administration sectors to make the necessary human and financial investment, to rescue both *Gaeilge* and its associated literary culture from certain death makes the latter inescapable. If administrators are in doubt regarding the most efficacious way to mobilize readers of *Gaeilge* to save Irish-language literary culture, publishers, educationalists and writers consulted could easily tell them what needs urgently to be done.

To repeat: such a policy vacuum regarding the survival of a presently weak minority language, such as Irish, leads inevitably to impoverishment of its ability to express the zeitgeist of the present era, in all of its dimensions. Instruments not adequate to purpose are abandoned. The logical result of such dereliction, is expressed mordantly by Albert Memmi:

"Only one natural solution is left; to write in the colonizer's language..."

In general terms, the printed word is still the necessary base of a modern society's information and communications pyramid. Anglophone print media provide that base at present for all Irish citizens of whatever linguistic background. Thus, the ability of Irish-language media, for example, to develop a uniquely Gaelic perspective on the eternal dialectic of old and new from their own cultural and linguistic resources is fatally eroded by the failure to promote real-life development of the Irish-language printed word...

Thence, Irish becomes confined, almost exclusively, to the leisure and folkloric spheres ("folkloric" as understood in the normal everyday speech).

However, a language cannot survive merely on the basis of its entertainment and fun value, its "quaintness", nor still less on the glories of its past. To survive it must rather become a vital, flexible, creative instrument in the intellectual toolbox of its users. In its own incomparable and satisfying way, it must keep open its unique window on the wide panorama of modern life, in all of its depth and diversity.

To seriously aspire to reach that pinnacle, however, a vigorous culture of the printed word is the indispensable medium.

POSTSCRIPT

"When I told a friend... that I proposed to talk about too long to an effort which is too feeble. the unparalleled difficulty before us, he begged me not to do so, saying that enemies of the language... would quote my statement for their purposes and ignore everything else I might say... Today I say without reservation what is on my mind, because I am certain that the only thing that might prevent us from saving our distinctive language and ensuring our own survival as a separate nation would be the mistake of trusting too long to an effort which is too feeble."

Ernest Blythe, 1949.

By stating the current situation of Irish and its literature, as I see it, so bleakly and bluntly I am aware that I can be accused of giving ample ammunition to the enemies of the language. So be it! The rubric of "whatever you say, say nothing that isn't a positive spin on the bleakest of realities!" is, at least partly, instrumental in bringing the language, its culture and its speakers to their present pass.

The latter thought puts me in mind of the reception given to a report on the state of the Irish language by Breandán Ó hEithir, the Inishmore writer and journalist, that had been commissioned by the then *Bord na Gaeilge* (the Irish Language Board, the forerunner of *Foras*). Breandán, a seasoned journalist and author, stated what he saw and heard in the Ireland of the early 1990s and submitted his report to the Bord for publication.

The facts, as Ó hEithir saw them—e.g. that there were only 10,000 fulltime speakers of native Irish remaining, were at radical odds with the optimistic official spin on unpleasant demographic data. The then Chairperson of the Bord, Proinsias Mac Aonghusa told me that there was no way *Bord na Gaeilge* could countenance giving such ammunition to the enemies of the language, especially the Language Freedom Movement. This organization was, at that time, campaigning against the State-sponsored revival of Irish.

When, as editor of *Comhar*, an Irish-language literary and current affairs magazine, I, at Mac Aonghusa's request, published the Ó hEithir Report in *Comhar*, official Gaeldom denounced the report as being inaccurate, unhelpful, if not idiosyncratic. It ignored the serious implications of Ó hEithir's observations and continued to this very day, to live in a cozy cocoon of fat-cat self-delusion within which seriously realistic strategies to save Irish were never generated.

To ask whether such a strategy is possible, given the omnipresence of contemporary Neo-Colonial Irishness, SCIS, simply begs the question.

In any case, the language shift from Irish to English proceeds inexorably in the *Gaeltacht*. The "half-way house" of *Géarla*, which has all but replaced *Gaeilge* both there and elsewhere in Ireland, is the end-result of self-delusion, willful blindness along with unrealistic and limited imaginings. *Géarla*, the Irish-English cant that has replaced *Gaeilge*, is hardly adequate to the task of re-establishing Irish Gaelic as a viable modern language.

The likes of the effort needed to arrest such a language decline has yet to be seen by mankind. Which is not to say that is humanly impossible. However, the will, intelligence and resources needed quantitatively to avoid the impending linguicide of communal Irish are not apparent to me in present-day Ireland.

Ach, i ndiaidh an uilig, níl léamh ar an bhfáistine!

TOMÁS MAC SÍOMÓIN

Irish Gaelic novelist, storyteller, poet, and journalist. A doctoral graduate of Cornell University, New York, he has worked as a biological researcher and university lecturer in the Netherlands, USA and Ireland. He was editor of the Irish language newspaper *Anois* and for many years was editor of the literary and current affairs magazine *Comhar*. His collection of short stories *Cinn Lae Seangáin* ("The Diary of an Ant") won the award for the best short story collection in the Oireachtas 2005 competition, while in the following year his novel *An Tionscadal* ("The Project") won the main Oireachtas literary award. His short story *Music in the Bone* was selected by The Dalkey Archive Press for inclusion in *Best European Fiction 2013*. He has lived and worked in Catalonia since 1998.

Other recent publications:

Raghallach na Fola/O'Reilly Hasta la Muerte (Coiscéim, 2015)

Is Stacey Pregnant? (Nuascéalta, 2014)

Three Leaves of a Bitter Shamrock (Nuascéalta, 2014)

The Cartographer's Apprentice (Nuascéalta , 2013)

An bhfuil Stacey ag iompar? (Coiscéim,2011)